MEMOIRS OF AN ANGRY SALES PRO–

Sales Leadership MUST Change!

Kimberlee Slavik

Illustrated by David A. Wiener

Foreword by To Be Determined

Dedication

People I know and care about are not going to want this book dedicated to them.

And those that deserve the dedication would sue me.

The REAL Dedication

Thank you to the wonderful sales leaders I have worked with. I've talked about several of you in this book.

David Wiener, the artist of all my books, was one of my all-time favorite Vice Presidents of Sales. When you get a good one, it's impossible to let him go! So I'm thrilled that we have figured out a way to continue to work together. He is still my mentor but now he is also my friend!

Thank you to the rest of the sales leaders. You have taught me what NOT to do and you are about to teach others the same lessons you taught me. And frankly, I hope you read this and learn something too.

I hope someday my husband will actually read one of my books. Until then, I'm grateful he supports something he has zero interest in learning. (Good thing he doesn't read my books so he'll never see this dedication.)

Thank you to my son, Zachary Steele Slavik, for the awesome book cover design. I know I am driving you crazy! Thanks for being a part of this journey!

Memoirs of an Angry Sales Pro

Sales Leadership MUST Change!

Illustrations by David A. Wiener

ISBN: 978-1-7331946-3-1
Library of Congress Cataloging-in-Publication is available.
Design & Layout by DynaExec
Published by DynaExec
Cover by Zachary Steele Slavik, CEO of Steele Cross Productions

Printed in the United States of America

Let's see who I will blame for poor sales THIS time!

"My most secure jobs and my biggest paychecks have been when I was an Individual Contributor in sales.

The least secure jobs and the smallest paychecks have been when I was a Sales Leader **working the longest hours**."

Why in the world would anybody want to be a Sales Leader?

Sales Leadership MUST change!
~Kimberlee Slavik
Memoirs of An Angry Sales Pro

Sales Leadership Defined –

1. People that lead Salespeople.
2. People that lead Sales LEADERS.
3. All C-Levels in a company.

ALL levels of Sales Leadership must change!

TABLE OF CONTENTS

FOREWORD

By TBD

For this first edition, I am leaving the Foreword blank because I haven't found the right person to write it yet and I don't want to delay the release of this book.

If you or someone you know is passionate about the way people should be treated in the workplace, please have them submit a proposed Foreword to me.

Here are the preferred qualifications:

1. Read this entire book and have strong opinions about the content.
2. He or she doesn't necessarily have to agree with everything in this book.
3. Propose additional suggestions how we can work together to fix what is broken.
4. History as a true salesperson AND leader, not just someone that sells a lot of books or does training.
5. Have a strong following and recognized name.
6. Respected and admired for his or her integrity.
7. Brutally honest writing style.
8. Able to relate to the content in this book.
9. Eager to make a difference and fix things.
10. Good at telling stories.
11. Humble and willing to share his or her own struggles, failures, and successes.

I will add the Foreword to the 2nd Edition.

PREFACE

What this Book is NOT –

3 WAYS TO FAIL
at everything in life:

1. Complain about everything
2. Blame others for your problems
3. Never be grateful

What this Book IS –

BAD MANAGER MISTAKES
that make GOOD people quit:

1. People don't leave their jobs - they leave their managers
2. They hire and promote the wrong people
3. They don't care about their employees
4. They don't honor their commitments
5. They don't recognize contributions and reward good work
6. They overwork people
7. They don't challenge people intellectually
8. They fail to engage creativity
9. They take credit for their employees work
10. They don't respect employee

Search – "Why Top Talent Leave Their Jobs" to see even more reasons good people leave companies!

**Together, we can fix what is broken!
But first we have to admit what is wrong.**

If you thought my previous books were too sales-focused or too scientific for your tastes, "*Memoirs*" may just be your cup of tea. It's full of sex, lies, cheating, scandals, villains, deception, lawsuits, deaths, conflicts, and more!

Just a typical day in the life of a Sales Pro.

But for every negative topic, there are mentoring tips, advice, inspirational quotes, funny cartoons, and proposed solutions to address and fix what is broken.

SALES LEADERSHIP MUST CHANGE and my goal is that this book gets things moving in the right direction!

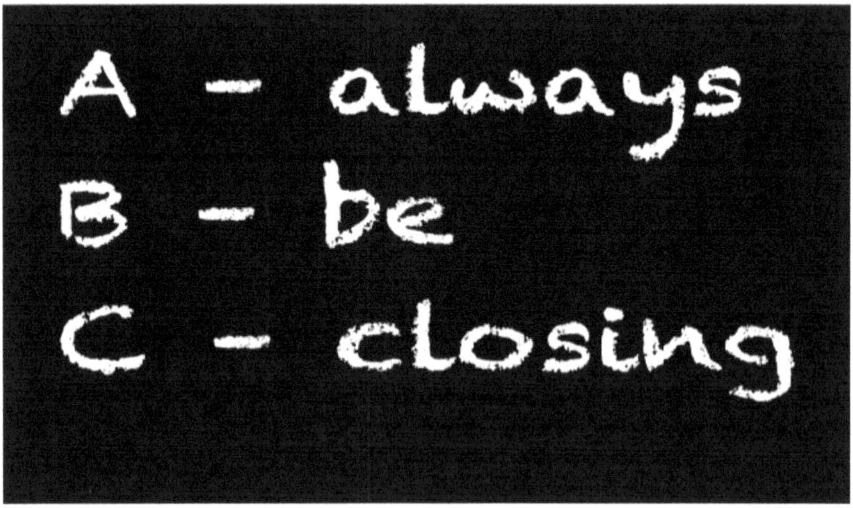

Glengarry Glen Ross is a movie that was released in 1992. It is considered, by many salespeople, to be the best sales movie of all time. And while it was intended to be satiric in nature, millions of people that have watched it apparently do not understand that satire is not real life because way too many of today's sales leaders behave like Alec Baldwin's arrogant and cruel character. So therefore cussing, yelling, belittling, and threatening salespeople have become normal, acceptable communication styles used to "motivate" salespeople to perform.

That IS the reason so many sales leaders are jerks, right?

Whatever has caused it, mistreatment of salespeople is way too acceptable today and for that reason, I'm sharing some of the stories I've experienced during my career as both an individual contributor and a sales leader. As you read these stories, keep in mind that I'm not even sharing the worst experiences! How sad is THAT?

This was not written to hurt anybody's career or get revenge; my goal is by the end of this book you will agree that sales leadership MUST change! I also hope that this book finds its way into the hands of some of the leaders I describe. Hopefully when they see their behaviors in writing, it will mortify them and help them see the error of their ways. In fact, I suspect there will be leaders that read this book and THINK it's about them when it is not. That is how common some of these behaviors are in today's world!

My parents not only instilled ethics in me from an early age, my first sales manager was also an incredible role model. I was extremely young and inexperienced when reporting to Mr. Ron Ackerman. He was incredibly likeable, very polished, well education, and well trained by Xerox. I know he viewed me as very rough around the edges, because I WAS! I viewed Ron as a father-figure, but after six years, I was eager to leave the nest and find my next challenge and of course, make more money.

I had no idea how good I had it until I left the respectful culture that Ron had built for his sales organization. I thought being treated professionally was normal.

Now that I'm considered a veteran in the sales world, I look back at the time I worked for Ron with much appreciation. Ron's influence early in my career became the foundation from which I built my professional reputation. Ron instilled fundamental principles that I am proud to say I have guarded carefully throughout the years. Ron taught me the importance of reputation, discipline, education, trust, respect, ethics, customer service, integrity, and metrics. I've had dozens of managers since we parted ways and nobody ever treated me with the same respect this man did. It's true that you never really appreciate what you had until you see what else is out there.

Mentor Tip for Fellow Sales Pros –
"Your Reputation and Your Brand Are Your Legacy. Guard Them Carefully."
~ Kimberlee Slavik, Author of Memoirs of An Angry Sales Pro – Sales Leadership MUST change!

Ron is now retired and the business world lost a great leader. The older I get, the less focus I see today on "doing the right thing." Yet each day I strive to continue his legacy by building & leading sales organizations with the same fundamental principles he taught me.

Like Ron, I am very serious about replicating success and helping those around me (including senior leadership, peers, coworkers, clients, and direct reports) reach their fullest potential.

Inspirational Quote –

"You are a true success when you help others be successful."

I have a sincere concern for people and enjoy helping people succeed. Because I believe people are the most valuable asset of an organization, I treat each person with respect. I WANT to be in front of clients and I want to sell with my team. Furthermore, I would never expect someone to do something that I am not willing to do, so I strive to lead by example.

Sadly, because of these traits and priorities, I don't consider myself a traditional leader in today's world. Where are all the sales leaders today with this approach to managing sales organizations? Why am I a minority with this approach? I've actually been told that this type of leadership style is considered to be **WEAK**!

Today's Sales Leadership MUST change!

Sales Leadership is a huge topic and if I were deciding if I wanted to read this book or not, I would be very interested in the Author's credentials. So let me just state this disclaimer – **I am far from perfect.** And I can tell you that I've learned from each of my mistakes and have grown more from the painful experiences than the good ones. People say that our battle scars make us stronger. I agree - to a point. **There are more positive ways to become stronger than from battle scars caused by the companies we represent.**

Mentor Tip for Fellow Sales Leaders –
SERVANT HEART
"If I help others surpass their goals, I ultimately surpass my own."
~Kimberlee Slavik

I've been told that the military breaks people down so they can build them into a stronger version of themselves. Sales careers are NOT the military. In fact, the sales leaders that I've witnessed break people down totally skipped the "building-them-back-up" step of this process.

This book is my attempt at documenting some of the abuses and some of the accolades that I have experienced both personally and professionally as I tried hard to maintain my dignity, reputation, and frankly, my soul as a true Sales Professional and a human being.

I want each reader to feel as though you have known me for years. So

I will start out the Preface by sharing two extremely traumatic setbacks in my career:

Story #1 – I was fired.

The day I left this company, I printed the sales rankings listing me as #4 globally (out of over 550 salespeople). I was about to be #1 once two of my huge contracts were signed. I still have a copy of these rankings that I keep in my personal portfolio.

The two deals that were with legal awaiting signatures were worth a total of over **$500,000.00 in commissions**. These two clients had purchased from me at multiple companies and we actually crossed that threshold from a client/vendor relationship to a true friendship. They both despised the company that I was representing and frankly, instead of educating them about my software, I spent most of my time trying to convince them that the company was a "kinder and gentler" company than it had been in the past or I wouldn't be working there. I was actually trying to convince myself that this was true as much as I was trying to convince my clients!

In fact, there was a running joke in the office that people with big deals needed to be on their best behavior because the company tended to get rid of people right before their deals closed to avoid paying commissions. Some of the stories I heard seemed like Urban Legends so I was optimistic that this would not happen to me. But as a joke, I packed up my office and had a box siting on the floor of my cubical with my belongings in it. I told people that I was packed up just in case my deals did NOT close and we all had a good laugh. I will share more details regarding this story in Chapter Three but let me share the story that was told to my PEERS about why I was fired:

It was the last month of the quarter and the office environment was extremely stressful. Our company had an entire floor with workout facilities and they even had trainers come in to help employees. My cousin had just started her own massage company and she shared that companies were hiring her to come in and do chair massages to reduce employee stress. I told her that I was sure my company would embrace that too.

So I checked with security and he gave my cousin a pass to come in and hang out in the gym and offer her chair massage services. I didn't have time to go get a massage myself because I was too busy negotiating with attorneys, answering questions, and closing my two deals.

The HR lady just happened to be married to the man that approved the security clearance and she came to talk to me about my cousin and asked about pricing. She told me that she was going to get with corporate to get approval to add it to the wellness program. That was great to hear! My cousin won, the company won, and the employees won. I felt that I had done a good thing.

So imagine my shock when I was called into my manager's office a few hours later to tell me I was fired for bringing my cousin in during the end of our quarter. I was told that when the HR lady called corporate, that someone there flipped out and envisioned our entire team having a massage party during a critical month when the company needed everybody focused on closing business. The person at corporate demanded to know who approved this person to come onsite. Sounds like a legitimate reason to reprimand the security guy that approved the clearance. Right? However, when I told my manager that the husband of the HR Lady had approved the security, I learned that the paperwork he approved and signed was suspiciously missing. How else did my cousin get her security badge and card key access to the gym? I certainly didn't have access to visitor badges.

This was my first exposure to how disposable salespeople are in

Corporate America. Even top performers are not immune from a culture that doesn't respect salespeople. Was the company really trying to find an excuse to not pay me the $500,000.00 in commissions? Were they willing to dispose of a top performer to justify not paying a huge commission?

Perhaps there were legitimate liability concerns about having someone onsite giving massages, but wouldn't a stern lecture be more appropriate? Wouldn't they want to save a top producer that had never been in any trouble? I did go through, what I thought to be, the appropriate security approvals after all. And I had a couple of huge deals very close to being signed! Weren't they concerned the clients would decide not to sign when they discovered their favorite salesperson suddenly disappeared during a critical point of the sales cycle?

One of my co-workers called me that evening to tell me that the Senior VP of Sales sent out a mass email to the entire sales team reassuring them that my departure had nothing to do with my two big deals; instead they should learn from my mistake and don't bring relatives in to do massages during the quarter end.

There is a LOT more to this story; I will share some additional shocking details when you get to Chapter Three.

Story #2 – Hero Today, Gone Tomorrow

Six years after my first story, I made the biggest mistake of my career. And even though this happened over 15 years ago, I am still embarrassed by it. In fact, I can't believe I am putting it in a book! But if I am going to share bad behavior stories about other people, it's only fair that I admit my own shortcomings as well. It's important that the readers know that I am not a self-righteous person that is oblivious to my own faults.

I also want to leverage this disastrous situation to describe how I WISH leadership had handled the situation.

I'll begin by describing the setting: I reported to seven different VPs of Sales in just five years at this company. Each time one of them was terminated, I was offered the VP Role. Why would I want to do that? I made more money than any of them, I had job security, and I had a pipeline that would make me a great living for years to come. That VP role was the most unstable job I had ever seen in my career! I watched my VPs start out very enthusiastic and confident, only to get beaten into submission before they were finally terminated. No thank you!

While all of those VPs were terminated, at least two of them did not deserve it and there were lawsuits that were filed. I was aware of the suits but they didn't affect me and I was blissfully happy because I was earning commission checks almost every month ranging between $38k - $191k (on top of my six-figure base salary). I was the number one salesperson globally three years in a row and I had just won another CEO award for being the most profitable employee as well. Life was GREAT! I had no intention to ever leave this company.

We had a Senior VP of Sales that was a very aggressive and verbally abusive leader. I had heard him unleash his wrath on underperforming salespeople multiple times in the past but because I was the top producer, he typically treated me fairly well. Actually, he pretty much ignored me because he was so busy beating up the underperforming salespeople.

But one day, we were on a call with some other people and he was drilling me extremely hard for not being more aggressive with my best client. Frankly, it felt as though he was putting on a show at my expense for the other people on the call so I tried to play along with his game to make him look good. But I'm also no wimp and I stood up to him multiple times and that made him become extremely hostile towards me.

I warned him that being overly aggressive could blow the entire deal and he said he didn't believe me. He discounted me when I told him that I had a great relationship with the client. I reassured him that we had been working together for several years and that I had things under control. In fact, I had recently received a $190,512.00 and a $120,650.00 commission check from two previous transactions with this client so I wasn't new to their buying process and I felt that I had proven my ability to close multi-million-dollar contracts.

Yet he wouldn't let up the pressure he was putting on me to get the deal closed sooner. So I offered to get the client on the phone and have the client tell him directly what the status was and why the multi-million-dollar contract wasn't signed yet. He took me up on the offer and asked me to connect the client to our call. I used the phone in my home office and leveraged the three-way conference feature. But when I called him, I got his voicemail so I hung up and got back with the Senior VP, who was now extremely emotional and yelling at me.

I pushed back and I wish I could remember everything I said. I do recall defending myself and I said something about the client negotiates for a living and he knows what he is doing and I am not worried about any of the games he may be playing with me.

Then suddenly, there was a recording that said, "You have reached the maximum allowed time for recording. You will be disconnected now." I knew instantly what had happened; I had not held the receiver down long enough to hang up when I tried to conference him in earlier! So our entire argument had been recorded on his voice mail! The client was going to hear every word of our discussion that took place after I got his out-of-office recording.

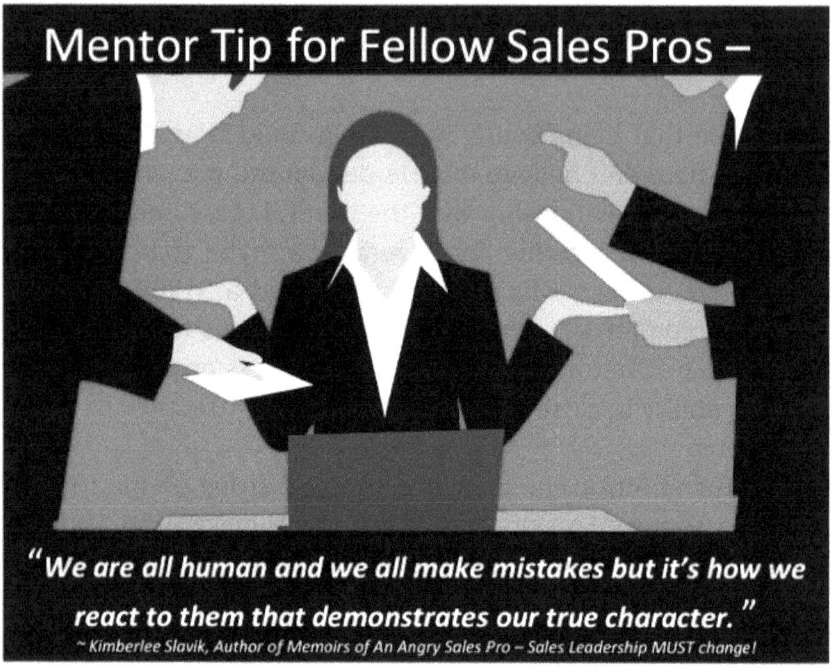
Mentor Tip for Fellow Sales Pros –
"We are all human and we all make mistakes but it's how we react to them that demonstrates our true character."
~ Kimberlee Slavik, Author of Memoirs of An Angry Sales Pro – Sales Leadership MUST change!

I was physically sick to my stomach and immediately started replaying the conversation in my head. I wish I could have heard the actual recording that my client heard but regardless of what was said, I take 100% accountability for not disconnecting that third line properly. Nothing anybody had to say to me could make me feel worse than I already felt.

What added to my anguish was that the CEO that had personally recognized my sales achievements, showered me with sales awards, eagerly paid me multiple five and six figure commissions, traveled with my husband and me on numerous achievement club trips, played golf with me, and told me repeatedly how much he respected me, would no longer even acknowledge me. That devastated me more than I can adequately express. Five consecutive years of exceptional sales successes, three years as the number one salesperson GLOBALLY, yet all those successes were suddenly forgotten and my image was destroyed during that one disastrous coaching session with my Senior VP of Sales.

The day after that fiasco, I received a call from my brand new (7th one in 5 years) VP of Sales. He said he was going to read something Human Resources told him to share with me. He explained that he wasn't going to be able to answer any of my questions. He was only allowed to read the statement from HR. It said something like, "Effective immediately, you are removed from the "XXXX" account per the client's request. You will no longer be allowed to have any contact with the client or any other client you have been working in your territory. Your current territory will be given to "someone else" and your new territory is now located in "a different city."

Basically, they gave my entire pipeline that I had built during the past five years to a brand-new salesperson and gave me an unworked territory to start over from scratch. My new territory was a three-hour drive from my old one. Nobody had worked that territory EVER; I would have to start from scratch building a brand-new pipeline!

These actions sent a strong message to me that the company did not value me or my client relationships. In fact, after five years of having a relationship with the client that heard the recording, I was told I would be terminated if I attempted to contact him in any way. I couldn't even apologize? THAT stung more than I can say.

What didn't add up is that the Senior VP wasn't punished in any way at all and as I recall, he was much more offensive than I was on that call. What added to my suspicion about the situation is that I kept hearing different stories of what happened next. One of the stories I heard was that the Senior VP, the one recorded saying offensive things about the client, flew to the client for a meeting. I was told he was the only person that heard the recording. He is the one that claimed the client wanted me off the account. He was the one that met with HR to ensure I was forbidden from speaking with the client. I've always suspected that the Senior VP threw me under the bus to cover his own behavior on that recording.

However, I will never know what really happened since I wasn't allowed to reach out to the client. And since the client never reached out to me, I wondered if something was said to hurt my relationship with him during that visit. Whatever happened, the CEO chose to believe the worse in me and he gave his full support to the Senior VP of Sales. Not knowing what really happened still keeps me awake at night. This is a great example of the "noise" (Chapter 5) that gets created in salespeople's heads caused by the company for which they work; and it is a career killer.

Inspirational Quote –

"The seeds of resilience are planted in the way we process the negative events in our lives."

~Sheryl Sandberg

The noise in my head was deafening so I ended up handing in my resignation. What I REALLY wanted to happen was to be begged not to resign. I had hoped that the prospect of losing their number one salesperson would incent them to reach out and talk me into staying. Instead, it was complete silence from all levels of leadership. To me, this meant that this is exactly what they wanted; they gave me a terrible territory, set me up for failure, and destroyed my motivation because they WANTED me to resign! I was so devastated that I decided that I never wanted to work in sales again.

During that one call, my most perfect job became my biggest nightmare and I never wanted to sell anything ever again.

What is ironic is that within a week of me leaving, the client was under some sort of government investigation and all deals were frozen. As far as I know, my huge deal never closed after I left. However, I doubt that I will ever know the real reason why.

That really was a difficult story to share but I wanted to make sure every single reader knows that I am not comfortable sharing some of the injustices I have witnessed during my career without admitting my own imperfections FIRST.

I also want readers to know that Sales can be brutal. It's an emotional roller coaster at times. It's HARD.

We need strong leadership to help calm the storms when they arise. We need leadership to encourage and support sales, not kick them when things get difficult.

Today, the perception of strong sales leadership is not what it needs to be. I hope this book can help change things for the better.

Despite the disastrous ending of this story, we grow professionally from painful experiences and this situation changed me forever. One thing is for sure, I have NEVER made that same mistake. I am now a master of many different phone systems!

It is also because of this traumatic event that I actually started to envision what it would be like to be in sales LEADERSHIP; I wanted to be all the things I needed and didn't get during this crisis. This event is the reason I fight for my sales teams because I know the pain of not having someone to support you when a problem arises.

Even with all of my success, there was not one person in the company that cared enough to fight for me or defend me. I have never felt so alone and unappreciated. I will never intentionally make another human feel like I felt!

What I WISHED had happened during this horrific situation is that the CEO met with me face-to-face. I wish he had respected my contributions over the past five years enough to sit down and talk to me like an adult. I wish he had showed some empathy by sharing one of his own mistakes and offer me encouragement that all would be ok. I would have jumped at the chance to visit the client with the CEO. I was eager to apologize and take accountability in front of both of them. Instead, the way this was handled was cold and obliterated any belief I had that the praise and recognition I received over the past five years were sincere. I still have the email the CEO sent just a couple months before this happened, praising me to the entire company.

Did you pick up on the fact that I still have my sales ranking report from the first story and the last CEO email announcing my latest award from the second story? It may seem odd that those two documents are so important to me. It is because both of these situations made me feel like I was disrespected and discarded like trash. Somehow those two documents remind me that I was actually doing a great job and they serve as proof to anybody that might question my abilities in the future. It's a sad world when the company and people you work so hard for can't give you those badly needed reassurances when you need them the most.

"HERO TODAY, GONE TOMORROW" is a sad reality in the world of sales. This HAS to change.

The primary objective for sharing my stories is to help others work through their own experiences and to offer suggestions how sales could and should be treated with more respect. As readers of my other books know well, I LOVE interacting with my readers. I look forward to hearing ideas how we can work together to help improve sales as a profession.

Mentor Tip for Fellow Sales Leaders –
BE SINCERE
"Respect is how to treat everyone, not just those you want to impress."
~Richard Branson

DISCLAIMER – As I circulated a draft of this book for feedback, it created different and passionate reactions. So I want to properly prepare readers for what to expect:

There may be times you want to throw this book in the trash and there may be times that you want to send virtual high-fives to me.

Brace yourself for an emotional roller coaster.

One of the readers of the draft had extreme heartburn over my comments about mandating office time for sales. The key word here is MANDATE. The point of this is if you let your employees know that you hired them because you trust them to know what needs to be done, it will be a huge morale booster.

However, if you hire them and then treat them as though they are too stupid to figure out when they should come to the office, you may destroy your relationship with them. And with legendary cultures at companies like Google and Box that have a reputation for empowering and valuing their employees, you may have a difficult time attracting and keeping top talent. You have to TRUST employees to know what they need to do to be successful. The good ones WILL do the right thing. And forcing the bad ones into an office isn't going to solve your real problem!

If you find yourself feeling angry, annoyed, or defensive over what you are reading, that is a NORMAL reaction; especially if you think someone is saying you are doing things wrong today.

Now think about this...you hire superstar salespeople and then start telling them how to behave, why would you be shocked if they have the same reaction? Nobody enjoys being told they are running their business wrong. And companies make a huge mistake by hiring top talent and then treating them as though they are incompetent. NOTE: Even if that is not the intention, their PERCEPTION is their REALITY!

Adding to these struggles is that very few sales leaders today are given the opportunity to make a difference because they are not empowered to do what needs to be done!

Neuroscience has taught me how to trigger emotions. A lot of this book is written in a specific way to get a reaction. Which I am NOT comfortable doing by the way. But there is a very important reason I WANT you to feel strong emotions as you read this book; an extremely smart person told me once that nobody can make you feel any emotions because YOU are the only person that can control how you react. So take those emotions and use them for GOOD! It's up to you to channel those emotions to be CONSTRUCTIVE versus DESTRUCTIVE.

Sometimes it takes strong emotions to trigger our desire to change.

A neuroscientist told me that readers that view salespeople as necessary evils (X management styles) will get angry and argumentative over some of the topics in this book. While people SUBJECTED to X management styles and those with a "sales friendly culture" will eagerly give the book five-star ratings. He told me to be prepared to see horrible AND great reviews of this book because that is what I was going to get. So I'm bracing myself for extreme opposite reactions.

Sales Leadership is not easy! If it were, we would all agree on universally effective ways to manage sales organizations.

Please proceed with an open mind and please don't stop reading when you get angry.

Also, brace yourself!
Because both of these stories about my career mishaps have huge twists. I suspect when you read the rest of the details, your perspective may change completely!

INTRODUCTION

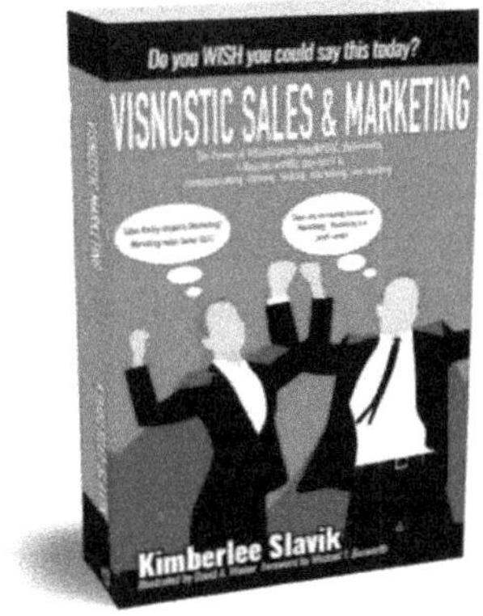

Visnostic Selling has been replaced by a bigger and better version called ***Visnostic Sales and Marketing***. This second edition is the first of a three-book series that covers sales execution, sales leadership, and the importance of post sales efforts. The first edition was released February 1, 2019 is a fun and positive book full of interactive lessons and over 70 graphics and original cartoon artwork by David Wiener. ***Visnostic Sales and Marketing*** includes incredible reader success stories from the first few months the first edition was available. Mike Bosworth, author of the best-selling books, *Solution Selling*, *Customer Centric Selling*, and *What Great Salespeople Do*, wrote the Forewords in both editions.

The content of ***Visnostic Sales and Marketing*** includes specific innovative sales **EXECUTION** tips that have never been described in any previous business or sales books. It also describes how to create a very powerful sales tool that will transform product-focused selling into a much-improved client-centric sales approach. The content is very scientific and is based upon powerful neuroscience tactical execution techniques. All of the books in the *Visnostic Series* have the power to immediately increase sales, drastically change lives, improve client satisfaction, AND improve the way companies do business!

Memoirs of an Angry Sales Pro – Sales Leadership MUST Change! is very different. It is the second book that focuses on sales **LEADERSHIP**, which will be much more controversial; it exposes several ugly topics around sales leadership that need a major overhaul. It is a darker and more aggressive subject. Yet I hope the stories are entertaining and the readers not only feel the passion I have on each subject, but will understand WHY and HOW we can work together to make a positive difference to the number one career in the country.

While I will share real life stories, I will omit names to protect the guilty and avoid legal ramifications. I'm not here to cause problems or get some sort of revenge, I will make points in the most passionate way I can so it will cause discussions and debates that will improve current processes, procedures, and behaviors in as many companies as possible.

In an attempt to counteract the negativity, you will see cartoons throughout the book that make fun of the problems I am describing. I am also sharing various tips and advice for both Sales Pros AND Sales Leaders that I hope inspire us all to be better at this crazy thing called Sales.

In both the cartoons and the advice graphics, you will notice that there are no faces. In fact, you have probably noticed that none of my book covers have faces either. This has been done intentionally. And yes, this is more neuroscience stuff; your brain should intuitively envision the faces of people you know on each of the characters so that each cartoon becomes a personalized scenario. Furthermore, without a face, you should be more focused on the setting and the other details in each cartoon.

I am also including inspirational quotes that I have shared on twitter throughout the years. One way I personally have dealt with negativity during my career was to search for something uplifting to counter any challenging feelings I was experiencing. I also admit that it is probably a bit passive-aggressive in that I always hoped that the person causing me the pain would read my posts and miraculously change their ways. THAT never happened but posting positive things when I was feeling bad has been an extremely effective way of staying positive and motivated despite poor leadership styles. I highly recommend you try it.

I really worried about writing this book because so many people expressed concern that this would make me look like I was being vindictive. I was even told this would destroy my career because people won't want to hire someone that may write a book about them or their company someday. But as an eternal optimist, I envision a completely different scenario:

I DO expect that company leaders that micromanage and terrorize their employees, will absolutely hate this book and everything about the author. This will not break my heart. Philosophically, if we are on opposite ends of the spectrum, I wouldn't want to work with those companies or their leaders anyway. In fact, I hope this book becomes a type of filter to ensure I partner with the right cultures and the right leadership in the future.

If this book inspires change, I will revel in the fact that the world will be a better place for future generations. If it helps GOOD companies become GREAT companies or if it inspires companies to make improvements, then this is a huge win for all concerned.

Furthermore, I'm still looking for my "unicorn" and I hope this book can help separate the bad sales cultures from the good ones. When I envision these possibilities, it is worth the other risks. After all, why would I want to work for a company that feared me after reading this book?

During a recent podcast, the interviewer asked me why my books are different than all the other books out there. And my response was that I am not a writer. Nor will I allow an editor to change my words. I write like I talk. I am a sales pro to the core and I am all about interacting with YOU, the readers!

If this book gets you fired up, if you want to share your own story, or you just want to talk about something, I want to hear you! **Contact me at Memoirs@dynaexec.com!** With your permission, I hope to include your stories and suggestions in future editions of my books!

I suspect that "*Memoirs*" will end up on many Sales Leaders' desks anonymously. If that happens to you, please take the hint as constructive feedback. I hope it opens eyes to how counterproductive it is to disrespect or mistreat salespeople, sales leaders, or ANY other human being!

As an eternal optimist,
I believe most people are inherently GOOD
and therefore are blind to their mistakes.
I hope reading some of these stories
will open some eyes to areas
in which all leaders can improve.

I want to clarify something before we get started; I tell a LOT of stories! You may even find yourself thinking "OMG this woman has QUIT a LOT of jobs!" There are basically three large companies that have at least six stories each and three smaller ones that often share the exact same issues. But the way in which I tell my stories, one huge story may spread out over six or more chapters. I will keep saying "The reason I left was..." The reality is that I rarely left a company for just ONE reason.

People that read the draft actually made a game out of it; they tried to figure out which stories are about the same company or the same horrible sales leader. Here is a hint - there are three horrific leaders that most of this book is about. And the terrifying thing is that all three are still in leadership roles today despite leaving a trail of destruction everywhere they go.

I'm sure many readers will think I'm actually writing about their current leaders. That is because most of these problems are universal in nature which is why WHO I am writing about is not relevant.

The companies I am writing about are also unimportant because these issues are not isolated instances. Abuse in Corporate America is rampant and Sales Leadership MUST change! In fact, I'm sure non-sales professionals will be able to relate to many of these issues as well!

At the beginning of the book, I have two graphics that describe what *Memoirs* IS about and what it is NOT about. I want to reiterate that this is not just about complaining and whining and feeling sorry for salespeople. And while almost every company has that one person that loves to point out weaknesses and constantly complains what is broken. I am not that type of person.

It would be pointless to write a book that just points out what is broken without offering potential solutions. Therefore I will make every effort to identify problems AND offer suggestions how we can work together to change leadership in order to make sales a more respected profession.

It is critical that the targeted readers, which are Chief "X" Officers representing ALL functional roles, Sales Vice Presidents, Chief Revenue Officers, and first level sales managers know how common and destructive these behavioral problems are.

My goal is that this is not a book full of isolated issues around one individual. Therefore, the more stories that can be shared, the more likely this book will trigger the change that is so badly needed.

Is there a topic that needs to be added that you don't see here? **Please send me your stories ASAP to Memoirs@dynaexec.com**! When you email or message your contributions, it's important that your story includes the following information:

1. **What chapter topic would your story address?**
2. **Identify a problem that needs to be solved.**
3. **Provide several proposed solutions to the problem.**
4. **Would you like to be credited in the book or would you prefer to be anonymous? Please note that no company names will be used in this book.**

Together, we can make sales a more respected profession!

Mentor Tip for Fellow Sales Pros –
"For Every Problem You See, Find A Solution."
~ Kimberlee Slavik, Author of Memoirs of An Angry Sales Pro – Sales Leadership MUST change!

CHAPTER 1
The Psychology of Sales – Sales is NOT a Necessary Evil!

Hey, I need you to go out and find me a salesperson! I'm in a bad mood and need someone to yell at!

PROBLEM IDENTIFIED –
Salespeople are not respected.

Did you know that the average career tenure for a Vice President of Sales in Silicon Valley is now less than ONE YEAR? Just a few years ago, it was eighteen months. There is something seriously wrong and we are just scratching the surface of what needs to change.

Ask any parent what he or she dreams for their children to do when they grow up and rarely, if ever, will they say that they want their beloved children to grow up and become salespeople. In contrast, a lot of them say they would love their children to become a doctor or an attorney. I think we would agree that ALL parents hope that their children grow up to do what they LOVE. How many salespeople do you know that LOVE their jobs? If you can't say "Most of them," we have identified a symptom of a much larger problem in the sales profession.

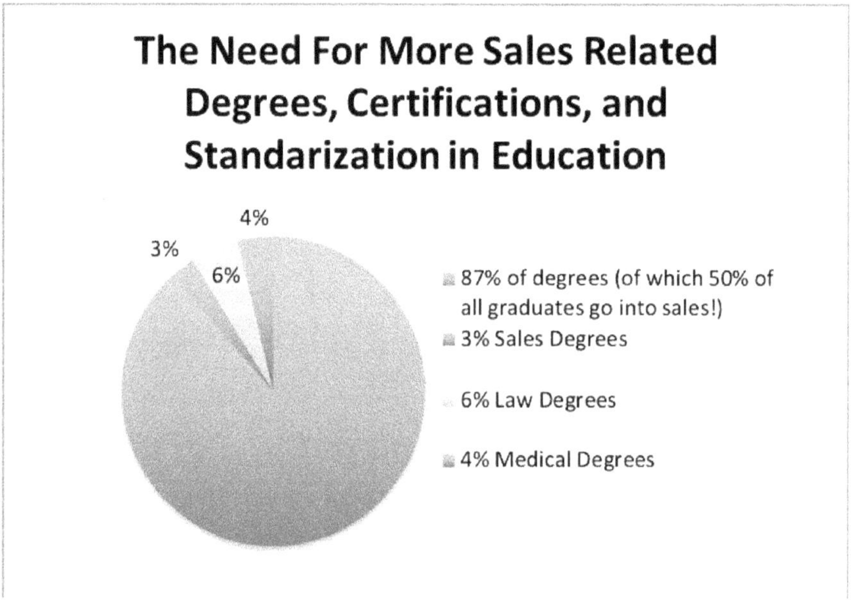

There are over 4100 Universities in the United States and about 120 have sales related degrees. This means that less than three percent of our colleges offer sales degrees. Yet over 14.5 million people have sales careers. **This math makes no sense.**

In contrast, there are 237 law schools in the US and by 2011, the annual production of law degrees was up to 44,000, and with a total of 1.22 million active attorneys, the number of lawyers in the country had nearly tripled. In other words, there are twice as many colleges that offer Law Degrees than Sales Degrees. Yet there are almost 14 x more salespeople than attorneys. **This math makes no sense.**

In addition, there are 175 medical schools in the US and in 2015; there were almost 1.1 million total doctors of medicine practicing in the United States. So there are 55 more Universities offering medical degrees than sales degrees, yet there are 14x more salespeople than Doctors. **This math makes no sense.**

Recently, a college professor told me that regardless of the degree earned, 50% of all college graduates will eventually end up in sales roles! **This math makes no sense!**

Why are there so few sales related degrees when clearly, it is the top profession in the country? What type of message is this sending to college students and to society? Is selling so easy that degrees in this field are unnecessary and perhaps even undesirable? These numbers are definitely evidence that this is a profession that isn't taken seriously enough!!

Due to the lack of education at the collegiate level, corporations are burdened to provide the necessary training for their new hires. Often, this is an entire college education worth of training crammed into just a few weeks. Why is the burden on Corporate America to properly educate sales organizations?

PROPOSED SOLUTIONS -

Universities are businesses and as with any other business, demand drives production. However, as was discussed, the numbers make no sense. If over 14 million people are salespeople and 50% of all college graduates accept sales related positions, yet there are only 120 Universities offering sales related degrees, it should be safe to conclude that **more universities should offer sales degrees.**

We must also acknowledge that parents are often the ones paying tuition and influencing career paths. And they rarely dream of their children becoming salespeople which may be the real reason only 120 universities currently offer sales degrees. It could be assumed that this is due to the poor image of salespeople. And therefore, **sales professionals need to elevate the image of the sales profession.**

Every salesperson should behave as a proud Ambassador for the World of Sales! If a young person is watching you (and they ARE), are you a positive role model or a bad one? Are you a person that others can admire and respect? If your children came to work with you each day, would they be proud of how you conduct yourself or would they be embarrassed or confused? Have your children ever seen you in a professional environment? How about your PARENTS or religious leaders? What would THEY think while watching you at work?

When I was young, I volunteered to work with Veterinarians because I originally went to college as a pre-vet major. My decision to change majors my sophomore year in college was 100% because of questionable behaviors I observed from some of the Veterinarians I got to know. Would your behaviors chase off potential future salespeople or would you inspire them to pursue a career path in sales?

Nirvana would be reached when young children begin to answer the question, "What do you want to be when you grow up?" with an enthusiastic "I WANT TO BE A SALES PROFESSIONAL!" And it must start with books like this one that blows the lid off of what is wrong so we can fix what is broken!

PROBLEM IDENTIFIED - Executives under-value the sales organization to most non-salespeople.

Imagine your company without sales. Unless you have a very unusual business model, there would be limited new revenue or growth. Without revenue, many current jobs could not be funded. Therefore, it is safe to conclude that most current jobs held at most companies are due to salespeople generating new revenue.

Mentor Tip for Fellow Sales Pros –
"Sadly, your company will rarely appreciate you as much as the competitors will."
~ Kimberlee Slavik, Author of Memoirs of An Angry Sales Pro – Sales Leadership MUST change!

I've had people ask me why I love being in sales. My response is always the same, "Sales is the most secure job there is when you produce; unlike other jobs that may experience lay-offs despite good performance. I would hate to lose my job because someone else didn't do their job."

The reality is that when sales are good, companies grow and people get hired. When sales are poor, people get fired. Yet when was the last time someone outside of sales thanked you when you sold something?

As you read this book, try to consider the differences and similarities between sales and attorneys. I chose to use attorneys as a contrast to sales for several reasons:

1. **Attorneys are a popular response when asked what one wants to be when he or she grows up.**
2. **Attorneys also require a lot of persuasion and selling in their profession.**
3. **Attorneys are right up there with Salespeople when it comes to negative stereotypes.**
4. **Lawyer jokes and Sales jokes are often interchangeable.**

Despite these similarities, most people respect attorneys over salespeople.

WHY?

Could it have something to do with the fact that you can get a Law Degree but must pass a Bar Exam to be allowed to practice Law yet you don't even need a sales degree to sell?

Could it be because salespeople endure more rejection than any other profession on the planet?

Put yourself in a typical salesperson's shoes. Per generally accepted statistics, to close a sale, a salesperson must contact TEN SUSPECTS to find ONE PROSPECT. And it takes TEN PROSPECTS to find a new client. That means a salesperson must contact ONE HUNDRED SUSPECTS to find a new client.

Which means for every new client, a salesperson must

face rejection from NINETY-NINE suspects and prospects. That is a lot of rejection for anybody to have to endure.

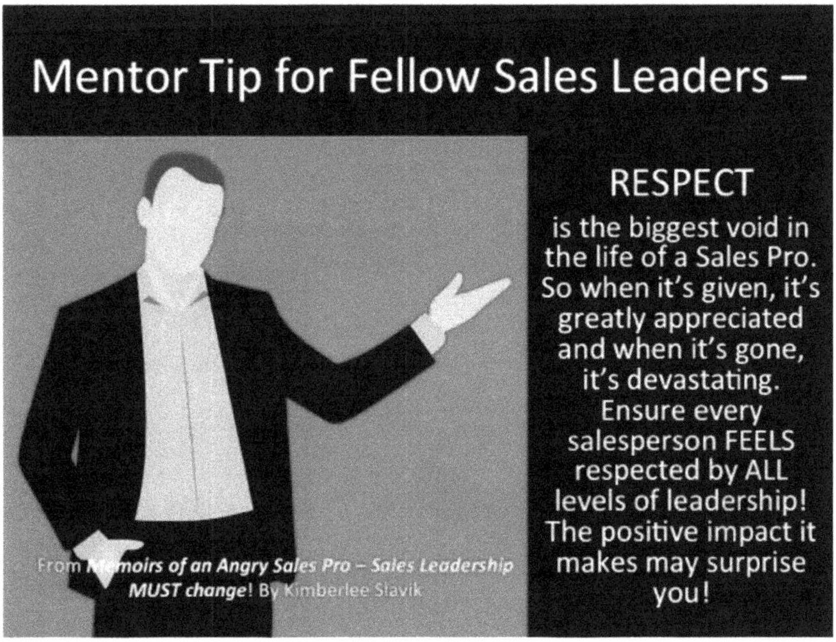
Mentor Tip for Fellow Sales Leaders –
RESPECT
is the biggest void in the life of a Sales Pro. So when it's given, it's greatly appreciated and when it's gone, it's devastating. Ensure every salesperson FEELS respected by ALL levels of leadership! The positive impact it makes may surprise you!
From Memoirs of an Angry Sales Pro – Sales Leadership MUST change! By Kimberlee Slavik

PROPOSED SOLUTION -
Leaders in every department and at every level should educate their teams regarding the value salespeople bring to their company! This simple gesture will help sales roles become more respected. In addition, it will help counter some of the damage caused by the lack of respect society has for salespeople as well.

Do you think it's easy to wake up every morning knowing you are about to face another day full of rejection? It's not easy or fun! But what helps motivate salespeople to face another day of abuse, is the confidence that their company supports them.

It's important for the sales team to know that other employees respect how hard their job is. It is reassuring to know that coworkers are behind them and cheering for their success.

In addition, salespeople need to know that the company is giving them the best training and the best tools possible so they face less rejection each day.

Mentor Tip for Fellow Sales Leaders –
SALES-FRIENDLY CULTURE
If you want to attract top talent you must first create a culture that top talent wants to be part of.

The goal of every "non-revenue-generating" employee should be to help sales reduce the number of rejections received each day. Every employee should be taught how they can help reduce the number of rejections the sales team encounters. There should be an incentive program in place that encourages employees to provide leads to the sales team.

I have proposed this at multiple companies and have been rejected almost every time. Leaders think employees should do this because it's the right thing to do. Don't be naïve; **COMPENSATION DRIVES**

BEHAVIOR.

Most companies pay an employee referral fee if they help recruit a new employee. Why not also pay a referral fee for leads **that result in a new client?** This would help the entire company "cheer" when sales closed some of the deals because more than just salespeople will be getting a little extra cash when new business is closed.

It will also help reduce the amount of prospecting and rejections that take place daily. People that reject this idea, are NOT a sales-friendly culture! You're paying ZERO percent on ZERO today. Why not pay an additional small percentage to generate revenue that wouldn't even be there without additional employees looking for leads? Maybe an employee has a cousin and her husband is an executive at a company that just happens to fit the perfect client profile. Knowing they could earn some extra money would incent them to make an effort they wouldn't normal make.

How much would you spend with third parties to generate more leads? And how good were these results? Employee generated leads are a guaranteed ROI!

Here is a good way to determine if your company is "Sales Friendly" or "Sales Inhibiting" - Go to your CEO and ask him or her if they have publicly acknowledged sales as the reason everybody else has a job.

Ask that same CEO if he or she has ever blamed the sales organization for falling short of revenue objectives to other employees. Ask him or her if they view sales as a necessary evil or as the most important organization in the company. You will find few CEOs that will actually admit they have a negative opinion about sales or that they have created a culture of resentment and hostility towards the sales organization.

Now go to the sales organization and ask them how THEY think the CEO will answer those questions. If the sales team believes the CEO views them as a necessary evil, they are probably correct. I've talked with many C-Level Executives that view sales as ineffective and failing.

**If a sales organization is perceived as failing,
a big chunk of the blame
must fall in the laps of
the LEADERS in the organization.**

What I have discovered is that CEOs SAY they have a positive culture for sales but their behavior often contradicts their words. An important thing often overlooked about salespeople is that they are intuitive by nature and they can "feel" a culture better than any other employee. Therefore, you cannot fake a strong sales-friendly culture.

One of the first things I do after I am asked to build or improve a sales organization is to go talk with the CEO. I want to see how he views his sales organization today, how he viewed the organization in the past, and what he would like to see the sales organization accomplish in the future.

Recently, I went to a CEO and suggested we develop a Quota Club for the sales organization. He immediately said no and that he would prefer to have a companywide event. This simple reaction spoke volumes. This man did not appreciate sales and did not understand the things needed to motivate a sales organization. Historically, sales had failed in this company and had a huge turnover. His response to me explained why.

He sincerely believed he had a sales friendly organization. But while we talked, it became more and more obvious that he had zero empathy for the sales profession because he had never walked in their shoes. Sure he helped sell some things but that is not the same thing as being a full-time salesperson.

Some of the best CEOs in Corporate America today started out as SALESPEOPLE! Some of the WORST CEOs I've seen in my career came from the FINANCE area of the business. Leaders with finance backgrounds typically cannot stand writing those commission checks. They are wired to view commissions as negatively impacting the profits of the company. Very few of these people are qualified to run a sales organization. Worse yet, without sales experience, they have no idea how to HIRE someone that DOES!

What leaders SAY is not what will resonate with employees. ACTIONS are what employees are watching and observing.

Poor Guy. Corporate said they have a sales friendly culture. So he shared his thoughts and they fired him.

Here are just a few personal observations that revealed what several companies I worked for really thought about their sales organizations:

1. Does the CEO criticize previous salespeople and sales leaders to other employees?
2. When people make mistakes, do they feel free to take accountability or do they feel the need to cover them up out of fear of retribution?
3. Does the company encourage sales to express their opinions, both positive and negative? Or is there fear in sales and a reluctance to speak their minds openly?
4. When marketing uncovers a lead, does it go to sales, to the "house" (i.e. Company), or to a lower commissioned team to save the amount of commissions paid out?
5. Does the CEO blame the company's slow growth on sales results yet praise and reward marketing?
6. Does the CEO have sales leadership represented on the Executive Board making decisions and giving input? If marketing is represented and the sales organization is not, there is a huge problem.
7. Does the CEO seem to dread speaking with salespeople directly or does he or she prefer to send messages through others?
8. Is the CEO engaged in sales meetings with clients?
9. Is the Top Salesperson on the internal Advisory Committee?
10. Does the company trust salespeople or is there a need to track them using technology such as GPS?
11. Has the CEO or CFO tried to justify not paying commissions even ONCE? This should be the happiest check paid out on payroll.
12. Does leadership expect sales to do "whatever it takes" to close an opportunity instead of having more concern about their

well-being and mental health?

13. Does anybody in the company EVER raise their voice or curse at sales leadership? Is it acceptable behavior?
14. Are the executives cordial to the current salespeople's faces yet talk bad about them behind their backs? This may shock you but they know when you do this.
15. Is the sales team forced to come into an office?

These are just a few examples of actual behaviors I have observed at almost every single company I've worked for. And during each interview process, every C-Level Executive insisted they had a healthy respect for sales in their company. I have wanted to believe every single one of them.

However, after just a few weeks on the job, the only person believing the claim that they respected their sales organization was the person making the claim. So let me add another number to that list:

16. Does leadership insult the intelligence of the sales organization by insisting the company has a Pro-Sales Culture when it really does NOT?

Part of this proposed solution is to be honest about your current culture. You cannot change or improve it if you are in denial.

PROBLEM IDENTIFIED –
Most sales leaders are not qualified to lead sales organizations.

Today, most sales leadership job descriptions say things like "minimum requirements are a few years in sales or sales leadership, an undergraduate degree is desirable, and an MBA is preferred." Sadly, none of these requirements ensure a candidate is qualified to LEAD!

I have had multiple sales leaders that were former football players. Three of them loved to yell and curse, and they often laughed while they did it. It was pretty apparent that they actually ENJOYED and entertained themselves with their outlandish behavior. One of these Shock-Jock-Leaders conducted weekly one-on-one meetings with each manager on his team and he started to yell at me again while discussing my teams pipeline. He seemed to truly enjoy berating me and he seemed to be trying hard to get a reaction from me.

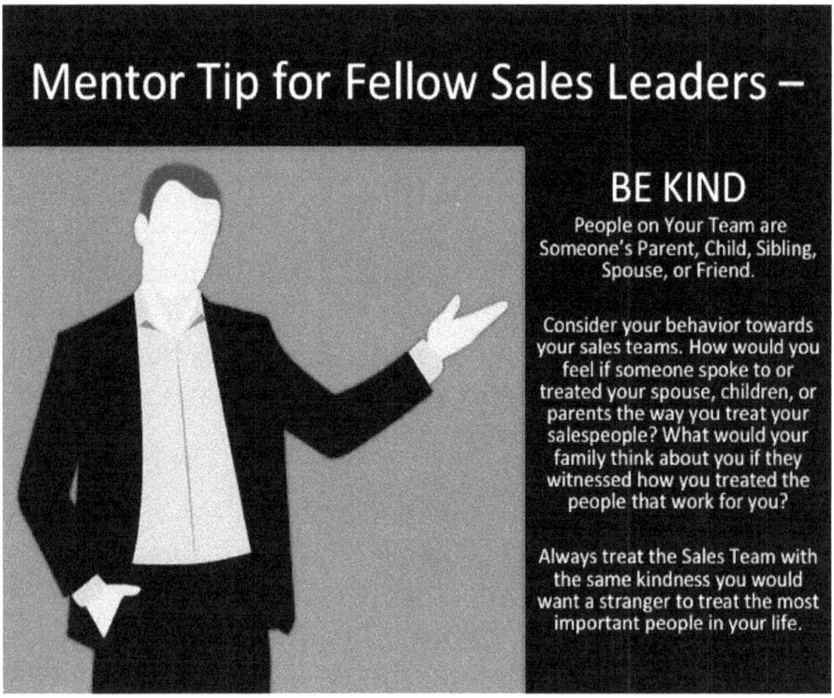

Mentor Tip for Fellow Sales Leaders –
BE KIND
People on Your Team are Someone's Parent, Child, Sibling, Spouse, or Friend.
Consider your behavior towards your sales teams. How would you feel if someone spoke to or treated your spouse, children, or parents the way you treat your salespeople? What would your family think about you if they witnessed how you treated the people that work for you?
Always treat the Sales Team with the same kindness you would want a stranger to treat the most important people in your life.

One time he got so close to my face that he was spraying me with his spit while he cussed at me. Everything about this man disgusted me. I hated working for him and so did everybody else. We endured it because the company paid us all well but he was a joke amongst his team and the other teams that worked with us.

After months of observing him scream and holler at other members of our team, I was numb to his ridiculous communication style. So when he was done with his latest rant, he stared at me and I just sat there expressionless and stared back. He said, "Well?!" And I asked if he was finished with his tirade. I then looked him in the eyes and said, "I get it. I've had football player leaders in the past. I can imagine that when you had a poor first half, during halftime y'all must have gotten screamed at to get your adrenalin flowing. I expect that yelling would get you so fired up that you would go out there and kill it during the second half. I understand that must be really effective during a football game.

But this isn't a football game and I am not a football player. I am a professional that expects to be treated with respect. I don't need you screaming at me to make me go execute. I need you to be civil and talk to me like a human being instead of an animal and have some actual constructive feedback or perhaps you could suggest a few new things I could try. What you just did damaged my attitude towards you and my job. I would appreciate it if you would modify your communication style with me in the future."

Inspirational Quote -

"You will continue to suffer if you have an emotional reaction to everything that is said to you. True power is sitting back and observing everything with logic. If words control you that means everyone else can control you. Breathe and allow things to pass.."

~Bruce Lee

I then got my things and left his office even though our time was not over. He sat there speechless as I walked out. We never talked about this incident and it was the last time he ever talked to me like that but that wasn't necessarily a good thing.

Another trait I recognized in all three of my football leaders was that they had an attitude of "win at all costs." So when I finally stood up for myself, his instinct was to "beat me" at this "game." Therefore, instead of taking my comments as constructive feedback, he upped his game and seemed to become even more determined to "beat" me with other types of mind games and super micromanagement tactics.

This isn't about me needing thicker skin; his future antics were wildly unacceptable to everybody in the room. But you will read more about him and his bad behaviors in another chapter of this book.

How does someone that treats people like this make it into a leadership role? I know for a fact that hiring athletes is desirable in the world of sales. I was a gymnast in college so I respect a healthy competitive spirit but hiring someone because they excelled at sports does NOT mean they can lead effectively. And hiring somebody with the "win at all costs" attitude can also be quite destructive.

I can't even imagine what type of FATHER or HUSBAND this man is as well. People like him need to be taken out of any position of authority because nobody deserves to be subjected to this type of abuse. In fact, I have observed that unqualified people in leadership roles tend to act irrationally because they don't know what else to do! I have found that **"Those that CAN, DO; those that CAN'T, RANT!"**

Mentor Tip for Fellow Sales Pros –
"You Deserve Respect. Be Sure You Earn It."
~ Kimberlee Slavik, Author of Memoirs of An Angry Sales Pro – Sales Leadership MUST change!

PROPOSED SOLUTION – CERTIFICATION REQUIREMENTS -

People that are in Sales **Leadership** roles should be certified. Real Estate Agents can't sell you a house unless they are licensed. You can't cut hair without a license. The preferred accountant is a CPA (CERTIFIED Public Accountant). After earning a Law Degree, you must pass a bar exam to be licensed to practice law in each state. You can't even dig a ditch to install pipes without a proper safety certification. Why in the world can any moron or jerk declare him/herself a leader and get hired to lead a sales organization?

THIS HAS TO CHANGE!

UNIVERSAL STANDARDS SHOULD BE ESTABLISHED -

There should be various levels of certification and standards set. For example, we all know that being a manager is not the same thing as being a leader. A Sales Manager Role is very different than a Vice President of Sales.

Therefore, different certifications should have different requirements. For example, a Sales MANAGER Certification may require prerequisites focused on sales skills. But perhaps a Sales LEADERSHIP Certification would require more psychology and HR training. I'm sure readers have their own lists of things that would make someone qualified to lead a sales organization. The question is how do we get these requirements debated and then accepted in the sale profession? Personally, I'm writing books, teaching, researching the history of other certification programs so I can replicate those successes, joining organizations, and becoming active on various boards at the collegiate levels. But I can't do this alone: I need every readers help! Please share this book and its message to as many people as you can and follow my lead! The more of us making these efforts, the more likely we are to reach our goals.

BAD ETHICS AND BEHAVIORS MUST HAVE CONSEQUENCES -
Just as an Attorney or Doctor can be banned from practicing law or medicine based upon their behavior or due to various types of abuses, so should sales leadership! Even hairdressers are at risk of losing their licenses if they don't follow sanitary requirements and safety standards set in place and enforced by health inspectors. I knew a very successful Dentist that lost his license to practice after becoming addicted to the laughing gas he administered.

INTERNSHIPS SHOULD BE MANDATORY -
Doctors begin their medical careers as an intern so they can work alongside experienced physicians. Why are sales leaders thrown into leadership roles without some sort of "shadowing" of other leaders in a company? Why do we continue to do things because they have always been done this way, versus doing things BETTER?

MAINTAIN CREDENTIALS THROUGH CONTINUING EDUCATION -
CPAs have to take continuing education and so do real estate agents to maintain their credentials. Sales Leaders should have the same continuing education requirements. I believe these standards should start being introduced at the collegiate level.

Let's start by getting sales degrees that actually mean something and become in demand during the hiring process for sales professionals.

COLLEGIATE LEVEL EDUCATION REQUIREMENTS -
Universities should create something similar to an MBA (Master in Business Administration). Why not have an **MSL – MASTER in SALES LEADERSHIP?!** And this training should include education components about corporate law, ethics, Human Resources, and Psychology so that each sales leader deeply understands the importance of the proper treatment and respect of other human beings! Better yet, teach them how to INSPIRE versus MANAGE people!

I was actually invited to be on an advisory board for a University in Minnesota this week and I hope this actually does happen because I plan to introduce this concept. If you have other suggestions, please be sure and email those ideas to Memoirs@dynaexec.com so I can bring your points up during board meetings. I hope this is just one of many boards I can join and start making an impact. I encourage each of you reading this to join as many sales organizations as you can and let's make this a grassroots effort to change our profession for the better! I am also currently exploring ways to get involved at UTD and other Universities with Sales Programs.

Think about it; would you rather have a sales leader that was certified or one that wasn't? Wouldn't you have more faith and respect for someone that actually came with some sort of FORMALIZED and Nationally Accredited Training? **Wouldn't you expect them to behave more professionally if mistreatment of you could results in them losing their credentials and their JOB?** I know I would! If you can't dig a ditch without proper safety training, why is it possible for incompetent jerks to con their way into a position of authority over another human being?!

Are you getting fired up yet?

PROBLEM IDENTIFIED –

Too many people assume that people that sell things are lazy and need to be prodded to produce results.

This leads me to the two famous Management Styles we have all studied.

Theory X managers believe that most people ...
Theory Y managers believe that most people ...
Are driven by monetary concerns
Are driven by job satisfaction
Will avoid work when possible
Actively seek work
Lack ambition and dislike responsibility
Show ambition and seek responsibility
Are indifferent to organisational needs
Are commited to organisational objectives
Lack creativity and resist change
Are creative and welcome change

The virtues and weaknesses of McGregor's X or Y Management Styles have been beaten to death so I'm not going to add to the long list of books preaching which management style works best. But I am including this chart because it summarizes and simplifies the two styles. I've had dozens of sales leaders; from C-Level, VP levels, to first tiered levels and each have behaved more like Theory X Managers when it came to how they spoke, treated, and approached sales teams. This is a HUGE mistake.

The problem I have with the X and Y theory is that it's too black and white. For example, I've always been "coin operated" but job satisfaction is almost just as important to me. I've had recruiters reach out with great jobs but once I heard the company name, I declined the interview because their bad cultures were infamous. Ironically, I could list several of these companies that were once on fire, but are now out of business or were acquired.

A negative sales culture may APPEAR to be working but it's almost always short term. The way you treat your sales organization WILL impact your company BRAND! And eventually, top sales talent will stop wanting to work for your company and it WILL lead to your company's demise.

The style of executive leadership actually impacts whether employees feel driven to succeed or defeated and demotivated. If you believe people are lazy, they will feel it and it will often cause them to lose ambition. Who wants to work hard for someone that doesn't respect him or her?

PROPOSED SOLUTION -

In my opinion, leading a sales organization is very much like raising children. You could have two siblings with the same parents, growing up in the same household, yet they can turn out completely opposite. Two different children could need very different discipline and coaching styles to be impactful.

Just as good parents will adjust to each child's individual personality and needs, good leadership should make an effort to understand the different needs of each person on the sales team and will modify his or her leadership style accordingly. This is not an easy thing to do. It is important to not appear to be treating anybody with favoritism, which is why ALL DISCIPLINE AND INDIVIDUAL COACHING should be discreet and should be done privately. Almost every single time I have been cussed or yelled at, there have been witnesses. I have even been told that this was done intentionally to scare the rest of the team into performing so they didn't suffer the same scenario. This logic is the epitome of BAD LEADERSHIP! A Bully is a Bully regardless of what title is on his or her business card.

Nobody should ever leave leadership's presence feeling bad about themselves. If you point out a weakness, give very clear instructions how to improve and be precise on what actions are expected and in what timeline those actions should be completed. I've had multiple leaders scream, cuss, and complain to me. Yet very few offered constructive ways to improve. Frankly, most sales leaders behave this way because they are not qualified to be leading. So they over compensate by screaming about whatever the latest problem may be because they don't have any recommendation how to fix things. Which leads me back to my previous proposed solution around certification and education!

When new salespeople are hired, they are almost always sent for sales training. However, when leadership is hired, what training do they get? Every single leadership role I started has sent me to the exact same sales training my team experienced. Only two companies have ever sent me to training to help build my leadership skills. And I want to acknowledge those companies – HP and Montare International. I'm still stunned and grateful for how much money Montare invested in me by sending me to Southern Methodist University to be certified in sales leadership.

When was the last time you have heard of a company paying for college level training for their people that are in sales leadership? It used to be very common. Today it's practically unheard of.

Mentor Tip for Fellow Sales Leaders –
TEACH
"Never stop teaching your team new skills."
~Kimberlee Slavik

NATIONAL SALES ASSOCIATION -

Can a company develop their own courses for a CPA? Maybe so but they can't create their own CPA tests. Sales needs its own standardized certification curriculum in order to elevate the image of the sales profession. Too many companies today have their own internal sales and leadership training. This leads to inconsistencies in the marketplace and these employees will take that education with them to their next role and their next company. What if the training was not a cultural fit at the next place? We need standardizations identified, documented, and professionally administered. How are we going to do this? The closest thing I have found is a fairly new organization called, "Sales Enablement Society."

How do we get something more "real" that would have the same credibility as passing a "bar exam" or becoming a "CPA?" Beware because most of the sales certification programs I've found are not credible. I have found several training companies that sound legitimate. However, when you look closely, these are just individuals that slapped a deceptive name on a company to make it SEEM like it is some sort of official national certification program for about $595. I've seen speakers and authors reference these certifications and it actually discredits them in my eyes because I know that if I paid $595 and sat through dozens of online courses, I too, could become certified. In fact, I could setup a program today offering to "certify" salespeople in Visnostics. How can these types of programs become "legitimate?" Otherwise, these certifications are about as valuable as a phony college degree.

I'm not going to include the names of these programs because I don't want to set myself up for a slander lawsuit. So I encourage you to search the web for "Sales Certifications" and you can see for yourself that there are several "speakers" that have programs in place. What makes them qualified to decide the proper content for certification programs? To reduce the risk of a scam, I'd like to see some sort of certification start at the collegiate level to ensure it is credible! I want to hear your suggestions!

PROBLEM IDENTIFIED –
Sales Organizations are constantly treated like a punching bag. At times, salespeople are treated as though they are the sludge of the company. And firing salespeople is a lazy way to address poor sales results. This abuse and disrespect MUST stop!

Once upon a time there was a Father that constantly told his son and daughter that they were losers. Neither child ever felt loved or appreciated growing up. The Father was a former low ranking enlisted military member and picked up in training that tearing people down was a type of reverse psychology that motivated them. The Father actually grounded the daughter when she brought home straight

A's...because one of the A's slipped to an A MINUS. This made her work harder to be perfect. The more the father criticized her, the more she was determined to earn his approval. She worked very hard as a child and as an adult to feel love from the Father to no avail. The result was that she graduated with honors in both High School and College.

However, the little brother witnessed how she was treated and instead of being motivated, he didn't see the point so he didn't bother trying. In fact, he actually believed the Father when he told him that he was a loser. The result was that he took two extra years to get out of High School and he never graduated college. Despite two completely different responses to the negative upbringing, one thing that DID come out of this destructive parenting style is that both of these children are adults today and both are void of any love towards their Father.

Would you tell your child they are a loser in order to motivate them to succeed or try harder? I'm guessing you'd be concerned about the psychological damage you would do to that precious child by treating him or her that way. Would you tell your child that you think he or she is lazy? How do you incent them to do their chores? If your child did the chores you requested, would you then come up with an excuse to pay them just a small amount of the allowance you had promised? Would you try to not pay them at all? Why not? What would happen if you didn't pay what was promised after the chores were completed? Would they still trust you? What are the chances that they would do their chores in the future?

So why would anybody think it's ok to belittle and abuse members of their sales team? Why would you think that you could dangle a compensation plan in front of salespeople and not pay them? Why would you think it's ok to change the compensation plan? This happens more times than it should. Why are you shocked when your employees walk out or stop working as hard? Why do you think it's so difficult to hire good sales talent?

I am so tired of being a sales leader and listening to the executives in the company talk about how lazy the salespeople are. This has happened at almost every single place I've worked.

"Compensation drives behavior" is one of my favorite quotes. If salespeople are underperforming, instead of jumping to conclusions or making slanderous allegations against them, why not consider there are things that the executive team can do better? Is your sales team "lazy" because they are demoralized? Are they battle fatigued? When was the last time leadership did something to INSPIRE sales to do better?

One of the men I mentored asked me to go to breakfast and bounce some challenges he was having off me. I accepted and I listened to him for 30 minutes describe how he has cancelled his cable, reduced his insurance coverage, had a strict grocery budget, and even refinanced his home because his sales were down. He told me that he had reduced his expenses as low as he could possibly go and has no idea what else he could do. My response was, "What plans have you made on how you can increase your commissions?" He stared at me with a blank expression. This man just happened to work for a company that capped his commissions. And you can probably guess what I think about capped commissions. This man was defeated. He had given up trying to get BETTER at selling so he was adjusting his lifestyle to his anticipated failures. Who wouldn't LOVE to sell against HIM?!

A demoralized team is a SYMPTOM of a problem. Be sure you aren't trying to "fix" a symptom of the problem versus the actual CAUSE of the problem. Beating a dead horse will not get the horse up and running again. Why not take a more positive approach?

While every person is unique and is motivated by different drivers, if you have salespeople that are not "coin operated" then you have hired poorly. I have yet to meet a salesperson that succeeded that wasn't driven by the dream of a huge commission check that would change his or her lifestyle forever. But there is nothing you can say to convince me that beating up a sales organization will make them better sales professionals LONG TERM.

Mentor Tip for Fellow Sales Leaders –
BE COURTEOUS
What Would Your Kids Think of You When They Saw How You Treat Members of Your Sales Team?
Behave everyday at work as you would on "Bring Your Kids To Work Day."

PROPOSED SOLUTION –

On what planet would anybody conclude that talking down to people, criticizing people, and not showing appreciation for people will make them perform better? As with the daughter in the story, it may APPEAR to work, but chances are great that these results will be SHORT-TERM. However, the long-term result will most likely be an emotionally exhausted person that finally walks away FOREVER. Do you want to retain your top performers? Of course you do. Why abuse them when things are not perfect? At no time should abuse be tolerated in a family or in a corporate environment. When things go wrong, why not show concern over salespeople's feelings and reassure them that things will be better? Why not share one of your own professional struggles and show some empathy?

The reality is that every human being is different. Therefore each person requires a different inspiration that will motivate him or her to perform. The key word here is INSPIRATION. Very few Sales Leaders understand how to inspire their teams because most of them shouldn't be in leadership roles. And when I refer to sales leaders, I am referring to ALL LEVELS including C-Levels.

I was on a trip with one of my salespeople and we were working with the Executives of the company. They were so incredibly rude to us. We joked that we felt like ex-cons at a diamond convention. During non-working time, the executives made plans and excluded us every single time. We even invited them to join US and were told they already had plans. During the actual event, their behavior felt extremely "High School" because they acted like they were the popular kids that were too good to hang out with the geeks. Even at dinner, they made a point to sit next to each other and exclude us from their side conversations. These were the same executives that put on quite a show a few weeks earlier by making breakfast for everybody in the office.

If Leaders don't act consistently with their employees in their humility and team attitude, EMPLOYEES NOTICE. The salesperson that was with me actually pointed their hypocrisy out to me and told me that the executives embarrassed and insulted her on multiple occasions; she couldn't stand their arrogance. I had come to the same conclusion but couldn't tell her that.

Executives need to have the attitude that they work for their team, not the other way around. And this attitude can't be occasionally!

Don't assume each person on your leadership team is qualified to help underperforming organizations. I have observed over and over again, when leaders are unqualified, they tend to get trigger- happy and start firing people and/or increase the amount of reports and micromanaging. I am convinced they do these things just so they can appear to be doing something constructive AND it buys them some time. I have been in meetings where leadership blamed declining sales on the new sales team and their ramp up time. This is hogwash! If you hadn't lost the previous team, you wouldn't have a new one! The sales pros on your team have seen this over and over again and this is when the resumes start getting updated.

NEWS ALERT – FIRING SALESPEOPLE OR ADDING MORE ADMINISTRATIVE WORK IS NOT A CONSTRUCTIVE WAY TO FIX POOR SALES RESULTS!

Instead of firing people, why not improve LEADERSHIPS performance and teach them how to actually IDENTIFY WHAT IS BROKEN so they can fix the actual PROBLEM?

What has your company done to help leadership at all levels improve their ability to INSPIRE versus MANAGE their people? This should be at the top of your list of priorities. I can't tell you how many leadership meetings I've attended that only focused on revenue and pipelines. On the other hand, in 30 years, I have been to **ONE** leadership meeting that focused on inspiring employees to improve performance! **ONE!**

Leaders talk way too much about the current revenue state versus actually demonstrating concern for the PEOPLE and their needs. How can YOU address this issue and inspire changed attitudes and behaviors towards sales professionals? How can YOU help those around you get more serious about making sales an honorable profession? This is going to take more than a Village; it's going to take an entire COUNTRY to change things!

Mentor Tip for Fellow Sales Leaders –
NURTURE
A bad manager can take a good staff and destroy it, causing the best employees to flee and the remainder to lose all motivation.

PROBLEM IDENTIFIED - Salespeople are not trusted to manage their time appropriately and must be watched at all times.

I worked for a company that was **rumored** to have installed surveillance software on every company issued laptop. If true, this meant they could turn on your camera at any time, they could leverage a GPS function to know exactly where that laptop was at all times, they could listen to your calls, and every single key stroke was recorded so if you happened to log on to a personal account from your work laptop, they now had your login information. The company also tracked the company-issued-cell- phones and could tell when your cell phone was at the same location as your laptop. As leaders, we could request reports that would tell us every single website that was visited and how long was spent on each site. If you wonder how is this legal, when the equipment turned on, a legal statement, that nobody read, popped up stating that the equipment and all data residing on the equipment was the property of the company; personal use was prohibited.

I only leveraged the reports one time. I had hired a new person and gave him ONE thing to do while I was out of the country during his first week; he had to learn a five-minute elevator pitch and present it to our team on Friday. When Friday arrived, he told me, in front of his peers, that he wasn't prepared and was unable to present. I asked what he did during the week I was gone. He told me that he was exploring our website. So I requested a report and saw that his first week was spent working for his previous company and shopping for real estate; he never once visited any of our websites as he claimed. I also uncovered that the only reason he had accepted our offer was because his first choice didn't work out . I was not thrilled to learn we were his back-up plan.

If you are wondering why he decided to use our equipment to do work for his other company, he did tell HR that he had turned in his previous equipment when he resigned but he still closing some deals. As a sales professional, I would have totally understood this and helped him if he had he been truthful with me. However, there was absolutely zero acceptable excuse to not being able to give a five minute elevator speech. This would have taken a sales pro no more than 30 minutes to master.

The official reason that he was terminated was for not presenting on Friday as required. I don't believe in firing people for making a mistake. I also believe when one of my salespeople fail, I have failed as well. However, this termination was 100% the right thing to do for me, the company, and even for him. I sincerely hope that next time he is honest with his manager because I would have been happy to work with him during his transition phase.

Inspirational Quote –

"I've always believed you hire character and train skill."

Lori Greiner

The decisions he made during his first week demonstrated his character, lack of ethics, and disregard for authority. He proved that I couldn't trust him. So why should I waste any more time on him? And let me tell you, this was a huge pain for me because I had to start the interview process all over again. Firing a new employee after one week set me back another SIX weeks from being staffed up in order to hit my revenue objectives.

Unfortunately, people like him are why companies no longer trust ANY of us!
So we are ALL being punished with various micromanagement and monitoring tactics.

My top earning years were during the 10 years that I worked remotely. I started my day at 4am and did all my personal things early in the morning and I was ready and in my office by 6:30 am almost every single day because several of my clients were on the East Coast and they were one hour ahead. I found 7:30am was a great time for executives to answer the phone. I didn't stop working until I was tired which was around 7:00 or 8:00pm each night. Plus most of the companies I worked for were headquarter in the Pacific Time Zone and I was in the Central Time Zone. So 8PM for me was just 6PM for my clients and sales leaders. It was just a logical thing for me to work these hours in order to make the type of money I wanted to make in sales.

However, Corporate America and CEOs like Yahoo's Marissa Mayer started preaching that for proper collaboration to take place employees must be in the office; the life of a salesperson changed overnight.

C-Level Executives are constantly being sold new and sexy reporting tools to help them make better business decisions but that data has to come from somewhere.

Did you take a close look at the chart on the back of this book cover? This chart is a collection of input from dozens of successful sales professionals over a six month period.

The general concession is that each day,
sales time decreases
while administrative duties increase.
It's alarming to us all
and yet appears to be an
invisible problem to the C-Levels.

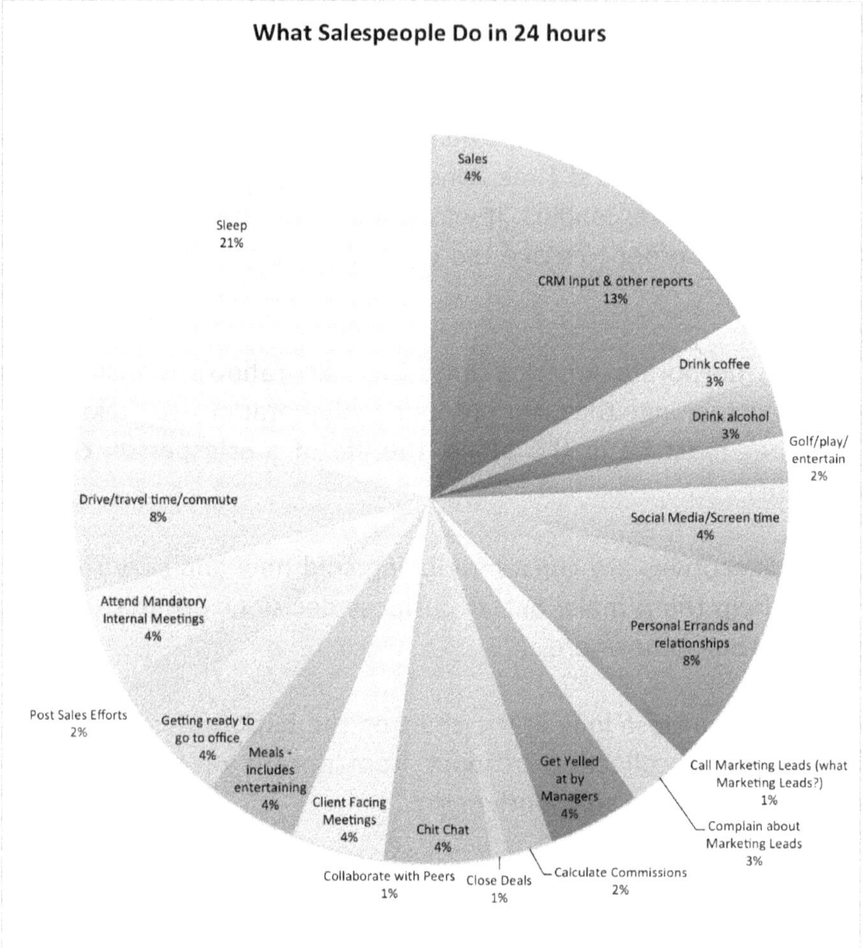

Time is the most important thing a sales pro has to manage so when someone starts trying to control how we spend our time, it can create chaos and resentment, which can be costly for all concerned.

Once I was mandated to come to an office, suddenly, my dry cleaning bills went through the roof yet my client visits went way down. Companies I worked for during what I refer to as the **"Pretend Collaboration Years"** lost 2 hours of productivity due to the time needed to get ready, 1 - 2 hours each day were now wasted commuting back and forth, and about 30% of each day was now spent painfully listening to coworkers gossip, talk about what was on TV, what they did or were planning to do for the weekend, birthday celebrations, impromptu meetings, various other dumb meetings, distractions from loud phone calls, and constant interruptions. These distractions filled my head full of things I shouldn't be thinking about if you want me to sell. MANDATING sales to be in an office is just DUMB AND COSTLY for all concerned.

Control is not Leadership.

Furthermore, despite keeping a can of Lysol at my desk and non- stop hand washing, I was constantly sick once I was forced into an office. I no longer had a sanitary work environment. I missed my headset, my fabulous leather chair, my quiet office with windows, walls, and a door. All this was replaced with what is called a "bull pen" which consisted of three cubical walls and phone with no headset, a plastic chair, and people all around me laughing and talking nonsense.

Bullpens send a strong message – "We don't trust you and we need to watch and listen to everything you do and say. We also don't value you because we have given you the cheapest and most uncomfortable work environment possible."

Once I was forced to go into an office, I actually stopped making phone calls to clients because I was embarrassed for them to hear all the noise around me. My clients stopped answering my calls anyway because the number that popped up on their screens screamed "solicitation" versus my name popping up on their caller ID. Needless to say, no matter how hard I tried to cozy up my workspace, my phones, office, WALLS, and chair at home were way nicer than anything the various companies I worked for provided me as a workspace.

In fact, you would probably be stunned how many broken chairs I've seen various salespeople forced to use when we went into an office. I often joke that if you want to find a broken chair, just go look in the sales area of any company. I might add that we aren't the ones that broke them; our chairs tended to magically get replaced with the broken ones. We should put stickers under our chairs and go find the people that actually broke their chairs. Sorry. I digress.

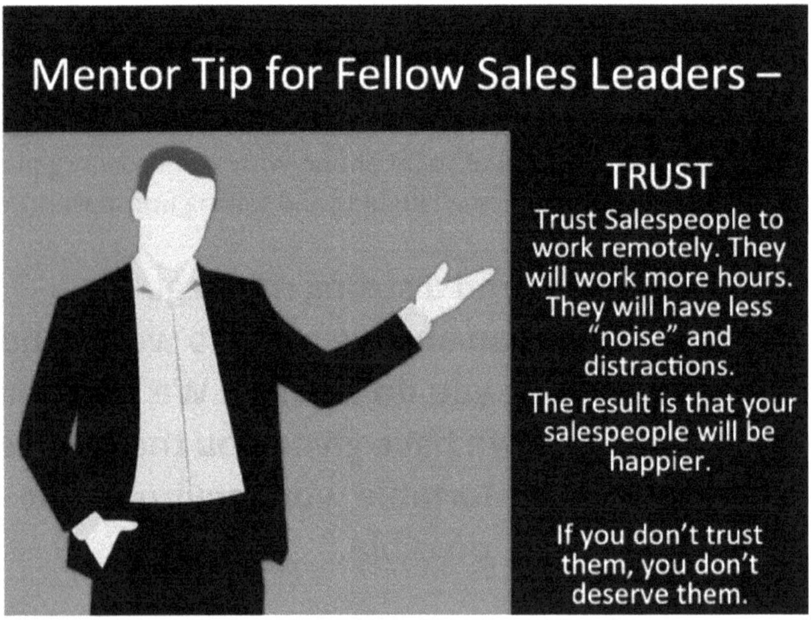

Mentor Tip for Fellow Sales Leaders –
TRUST
Trust Salespeople to work remotely. They will work more hours. They will have less "noise" and distractions.
The result is that your salespeople will be happier.
If you don't trust them, you don't deserve them.

I was much more stressed working from an office because now I had no work/life balance. When I worked remotely, I could start a load of laundry in between calls, and my bathroom was always private and clean.

When I worked for companies with office mandates, I had to leave at five o'clock to get all my personal things done. It takes a lot of time to commute, pick up dry cleaning, get a load of laundry started, grocery shop, clean my house, and cook dinner (Ok, who am I kidding here? PICK UP dinner.).

I also never went to lunch when working remotely because it was so easy to grab a bite and keep working. In an office, so I didn't seem unsocial, I ended up going out with people I worked with and spent another hour listening to whatever was on their minds. I spent an hour each day politely listening about their spouses and kids and their frustrations around work and life. I admit that I often used these times to vent my own frustrations as well, which just adds to all the distractions from selling. Rarely, if ever, were lunches actually used to collaborate. The reality is that when you force a bunch of salespeople together into an office every day, the venom tends to start spewing.

Nobody needs this noise in their head when they are trying to sell.

Having an office job made me develop a 7-5 mentality for the first time in my sales career. By 5PM, I couldn't get out the door fast enough and after battling for my life commuting home; I was mentally done with work for the day.

So my 14-hour days selling while working remotely were reduced to about 5 hours of selling…on a GOOD day.

So let's go back to the original problem identified so you can see the irony in this part of the book –

Salespeople are not trusted to manage their time appropriately and must be watched at all times.

This is a chicken/egg syndrome. Time is a salesperson's most valuable asset to manage. Yet companies, in their almighty wisdom, have decided that they must "help" salespeople manage their time by mandating how that time is spent. The result is that salespeople's time (and QUALITY of time) spent selling is being demolished. Go look at the chart on the back cover again. How much of those 24 hours are being dictated by companies?

THIS MUST CHANGE!

Mentor Tip for Fellow Sales Leaders –
BELIEVE IN YOUR PEOPLE & THEY WILL BELIEVE IN THEMSELVES
"Controlling is not leading."
~Kimberlee Slavik

PROPOSED SOLUTION –

This should be a no-brainer solution but most executives and sales leaders will attempt to justify this mandatory office policy by saying – "We don't WANT salespeople comfortable in an office because we want them in front of clients instead! So the more miserable they are in the office, the more time they will spend with clients." Can they actually hear themselves when they say these words??? Hello? You just said I'm too stupid to do the right thing so you have to torture me to make me do it!

Stop trying to justify this decision; NEVER force salespeople into an office. It's like taking an eagle and putting into a small cage; it's not natural and it's not healthy. If you don't trust your people, you shouldn't have hired them. In fact, if you don't trust your people, (despite what you want to believe) you are probably a horrible leader.

While most leaders I've met with this type of attitude are often the owners of the company, distrust can be found in all sizes of companies. Sales people that got promoted into leadership roles almost always felt the need to micromanage every second of my day. **I've discovered that those that don't trust are usually the ones that can't be trusted**.

If you work for an owner that insists sales comes to an office, there is no advice I can give that will change them. They will have to figure out the errors of their ways themselves but the chances of that happening are slim to none. So my recommendation is to never accept a job from a privately owned company that insists sales must come to an office. If they don't trust salespeople to know when they need to come to the office, they don't deserve you as their employee.

Once they can no longer hire and retain top talent (also be sure and give them a copy of this book), maybe their eyes will be open to how silly this expectation is for sales professionals.

The best salespeople think like Entrepreneurs and they want to earn as much money as possible, not talk about politics, movies/TV shows, why their sales management is incompetent, or celebrate office birthdays. **GOOD salespeople will actually FEAR and DREAD time spent in the office.**

Serious sales pros will resent when they are distracted from selling because you are literally taking money out of their pockets! If leadership doesn't have a full day of **constructive** activities that are intended to increase sales, why waste time and money for the company, salespeople, and leadership just to ensure they are visible? One day per week should be the maximum time for sales to be in an office. And that is only if there is a structured itinerary justifying the value of their time spent in the office. Just having people come to an office and expecting them to organically make their time productive is not a realistic expectation because of all the distractions and various people wanting their time.

Ditch the bullpens for salespeople! Salespeople are loud and outgoing. Put employees that have quiet personalities and quiet jobs in an open area if that is all you have available in your office. But hosting salespeople in an open environment, and then having other employees shush them for being too loud is insanity plus it causes unnecessary tension between employees.

And for Pete's sake, don't give authority to people that don't know how to properly lead, trust, and inspire their team!

People reading this may think that an exception should be made for inside salespeople. NOT TRUE. In fact, when I receive a call and I answer and hear others talking in the background, I don't even say Hello; I hang up immediately. Do you really want your inside salespeople to sound like a call center? Very few people want to take those calls.

Now I am going to appear to contradict every word I just wrote. You WILL have salespeople that have too many distractions at home and will prefer to come to the office. Let them! The point of all this ranting is that your salespeople are big boys and girls and will know what they need to do to make the most money.

Trust the salespeople you hired or the good ones will leave and the bad ones will stay and try and play your games. This is a recipe for low or non-existent sales.

It's ok to have rules for people working remotely. A great example of one of these rules is that you cannot have a dog around your office when on a call with a customer because no client should ever hear a dog bark. I signed papers at one company that said if you have children at home, you had to provide proof that you have a childcare provider so the child won't interrupt your calls with clients. Rules are ok. However, these expectations are important to set during the interview process, not after a salesperson starts working for you.

And forget the call reports and all the administrative work you will be tempted to pile on remote workers. It's a common practice to share our calendars with each other. I had no problems with the team sharing calendars because they understood that calendars replaced call reports. I could find out what I needed by simply taking a peek into their day, week, or month. The only additional data you should be focused on are the results or whatever your CRM produces. You hired them – right? Trust your decision. Trust they want to do the right thing. **Let them do what works for them until the results aren't there.**

PROBLEM IDENTIFIED –
The Sales Organization is rarely asked for their opinions.

This is a rampant issue in "Sales Is a Necessary Evil" cultures. If the sales team is not respected, why in the world would anybody ask for their input?

I will reference a term throughout this book. I call it, **"The Emperor's New Clothes Syndrome"** or **"ENC Syndrome."** And leaders at all levels better pay attention to it because it's a very costly mistake made by all levels of leadership today.

While leaders are obsessing over their reports, they are losing touch with reality. And I will discuss this in a later chapter. For now, just know that leaders are unintentionally becoming blind to things that are taking place right in front of them. It may be an employee that leadership thinks hung the moon, while the rest of the staff sees him as a complete loser. Others may be in denial because they put a program in place and can't accept that they made a mistake. Whatever is causing leadership to ignore obvious issues, it is making them look pretty stupid to their teams. This is a serious problem because if you don't know something is broken, how can you fix it?

This book is full of examples of the **ENC Syndrome** but here is an example: A senior level leader was demoted and a new leader was brought it. The demoted leader was expected to help the new one become successful. Employees witnessed multiple sabotages taking place. It was extremely obvious to the employees that the demoted leader had no motivation for the new leader to be successful. In fact, it was very clear that he WANTED the new leader to fail. Was it subconscious? Nobody knew that answer expect the demoted leader. But the employees were shocked that nobody seemed concerned that this was a potential issue. Several of us discussed how our various improvement projects were being modified and destroyed by this man. How could WE see this man was disgruntled and nobody else could see it?

PROPOSED SOLUTION –

Salespeople can be one of the best sources for reality for leaders. But leaders must first convince their employees that honest feedback will NOT be punished. Having an employee advisory panel is an effective way to flush out things that leadership is unable to see. There will be several more stories about ENC. But nothing will work until leaders create a culture where your employees are comfortable telling them when they are naked!

PROBLEM IDENTIFIED –

Sales LEADERSHIP is not taken seriously as a career; Sales Leaders are considered disposable.

Remember the statistics I gave in Chapter One about the tenure of sales leadership is now less than twelve months? One reason I believe this number is so low is because companies have decided that instead of paying appropriately for consultants, they will pretend to hire sales leaders knowing good and well that they have no intention on keeping them. Telling someone that you are hiring him or her at a base salary for $200,000/year is about $100/hour. In contrast, a consultant will be $300- $500/hour. So it is good business sense to pretend to hire someone permanently in order to get a big project completed, then lay him or her off when it's done. Right? Instead of a three-month project costing $156,000 - $260,000 with consultants, you hire a poor Sap "permanently" (for three months) to do the same project and it will only cost you $50,000!

THREE companies that had no intention on keeping me have hired me as a Sales Leader. They wanted cheap consulting so they pretended to hire me permanently, had me perform some major projects and then "laid me off." This impacted my resume in a negative way. One had me hire and train an entire sales organization;

another hired me to perform a competitive analysis. And the third one had me rewrite the compensation plan and setup their CRM system.

PROPOSED SOLUTION –
It's ok to need temporary help. But use a temp agency! There are great companies out there that provide "FRACTIONAL Sales Leadership" like my company, DynaExec, Beacon, or Sales Xceleration. Please don't mess with someone's career by being dishonest about your intentions.
https://salesxceleration.com/hiring-fractional-sales-leader/

Sales Organizations are highly fragile and yet are extremely critical for a company to succeed and grow. Treat them well and the rewards will be great! Treat them poorly and you are shooting yourself in the foot!

Sales is NOT a necessary evil!
Sales Leadership MUST change!

Inspirational Quote -

"Talented people are the most valuable resource in any organization."

Treat them as such!

CHAPTER 2 –
Give Us Something To Sell That Works!

*The World's Best Salesperson.
Eskimos love his special ice.*

PROBLEM IDENTIFIED –
"Fake It Until You Make It" is rampant in the business world.

By now everybody should have watched the documentaries or news about Theranos, the defunct company known for its amazing claims to have revolutionized blood testing using tiny traces of blood from a simple finger prick. The founder and former CEO is now infamous. Her name is Elizabeth Anne Holmes. She has fascinated me from the first time I heard her speak. She dressed like Steve Jobs in all black turtlenecks. Her voice was extremely low and I was personally inspired to see a woman doing such great things at such a young age. I can see why she was able to raise over $700 million in venture capital and built a company to a peak value of $10 billion valuation before it was exposed as a fraud and collapsed. Investors, journalists, employees, even politicians had their reputations damaged because they fell for the Theranos sales pitch.

The entire story of Elizabeth and Theranos reminds me of the expression, "That person is such a great salesperson, she can sell ice to Eskimos!" Whenever someone said this to me, while I knew they intended it to be a compliment, I was wildly insulted. Why would I want to sell something to someone that clearly didn't need what I was selling? That didn't seem ethical or even logical to me. But Elizabeth was most definitely selling ice to Eskimos. In fact, she was selling invisible ice because she sold something that didn't even exist.

Isn't that what most CEOs do? They have to "sell" to stockholders and investors. They "sell" to employees. But what if they had something that didn't work? Sadly, I accepted sales or sales leadership roles with THREE different companies that sold something that either didn't exist or didn't work well. I left all three companies after uncovering the fraud. And yes, I said the word FRAUD because each company KNEW what they had was bogus yet they hired people like me to leverage our client relationships and good reputations to sell their "invisible ice."

The best marketing, the best advertising, the best sales tools came from one of these companies. I want to share all three stories and then I will make a huge point at the end that may shock you.

Side bar – if you are trying to look at my LinkedIn to figure out what companies I am talking about in this book, don't bother. Several of these companies are no longer listed on my resume. Others are intentionally vague and have false hints so you can't figure out who they are. I respect your sleuthing efforts though because I would have done the same thing!

Company #1 –
This company had already received about 7 rounds of funding over a 10-year period when I came on board so why wouldn't I believe it was a legitimate company with a legitimate offering? I was hired as the National Sales Manager and began hiring my team. One of the first things I was requested to do was to get the device into a lab and have a competitive analysis run. I did this very quickly because I needed the data to help me sell these devices. So I was happy to comply with the request. Long story short (don't you hate that phrase?), the lab reported that while it worked as it claimed, it was 5 years behind the worst competitor. When I came back and reported the findings, I was told that my services were completed. These people hired me as a temporary employee but neglected to tell ME! I wasn't fired. I was told that the company was going to shut down so I was technically laid off based upon these findings. But it was no coincidence that I was laid off before the "warranty" period my recruiter gave them so they could request a refund of the placement fee. And yes, this company is the same company I described in the previous chapter that hired me as temporary help but neglected to tell me!

Despite this sudden decision to shut down sales, they kept one of the men that reported to me. This wasn't logical to me at the time but today I see very clearly what was really being sold at this company and who the real clients were. This company never told the investors of the lab findings so they kept operating a shell of a company. They also continued to ask for and receive investor funding. They ended up getting over $90 million and 10 rounds of funding before the investors finally pulled the plug. I still wonder today where all that money went.

In 10 years, only one device had been sold. It is highly doubtful that many more, if any, sold after I left. So what was really being sold to the investors was the VISION of a company buying their company. Investors were counting on it and gambled and lost over $90 million.

Therefore, Investors were the REAL clients. So the reason they kept the man I hired was to give the illusion to the investors that sales efforts were continuing. This is a great example of "Fake it until you make it."

I founded DynaExec (Dynamic Executives) because of what I witnessed here and my goal was to bridge the gap between investors and inventors. After all, Venture Capitalists are brilliant at finding ways to get huge returns on their investments but they aren't necessarily technology savvy and could be easily fooled. And inventors are proud of their creations and I believe they sincerely hope, dream, and believe they have created the next big thing. But inventors don't necessarily know how to go-to-market. So my goal was to bridge the gap between investors and inventors. If an investor hired me, I would do what I did for this company. I would perform things like a competitive analysis and tell them honestly if what they had was a valid investment opportunity. If inventors hired me, I would do the same thing and I would help them find investors and help build a team to sell their invention.

During my first launch of DynaExec, I was exposed to so many scams that it led me back to Corporate America to sell something more established that I knew worked. I have a whole new respect for Venture Capitalists. There are a LOT of Elizabeth Holmes out there making a great living selling a fake vision versus reality!

Lessons learned here – Buyers Beware is a very well-known saying but I now realize that another saying should be Investors Investigate! The reason this story is important for this book, is that us little sales professionals are just pawns in these companies and their little schemes. If they can trick billion-dollar investment firms, it's a simple thing to hire unsuspecting salespeople to add to their illusion of legitimacy.

My solution to this problem is to educate readers of this book about what to look out for so readers can avoid the same mistakes I have made. I was looking for that next big invention that would make me wealthy on stock options. Well, it hasn't happened and it absolutely hasn't been worth the risks I took. I hope to help others avoid these same mistakes.

Company #2 -
This was so brilliant that it is impossible not to be in awe over them. This was my own little "Theranos" experience.

First of all, they managed to hire the absolute best sales team I have ever had the honor to work with. I was an individual contributor but none of us were treated as "just a salesperson." They reached out to me personally. Somehow the VP of Sales got his hands-on sales rankings for every single one of his competitors and he called every person that was number one on each list.

The VP also insisted that each salesperson recruit their favorite SE (Software Engineer). This was another brilliant move on their part because when you are selling complex enterprise deals, the synergy between the "psychologist/salesperson" and the "technologist/SE" can be critical to winning deals. By hiring a proven and successful team, they won't have that awkward phase of getting to know each other and therefore will hit the ground running. Brilliant hiring move! I've never seen another company do this in my entire career. It just added to my passion and conviction towards this new career move. I hit the jackpot!

The compensation package was the best I'd ever seen. They didn't hire a silly company to do a dinky background check. This VP made a personal goal to try and find dirt on each of us so he did the investigating himself. One of the things he did was to pull a credit report and he made every single one of us show him our W2s to prove our earnings. He then called me to tell me that he wanted to hire me but there was a huge problem; I wasn't in enough debt and he didn't think I needed the money badly enough to be a top performer. Challenge accepted! I went out that day and bought a $100,000 motorhome and sent him the paperwork and asked it that was good enough. He laughed and I was at least going to the next level of the interview process.

The next step was to have dinner with the all-male executive team to ensure they approved. The CEO, COO, SVP, CTO were all there. We went to a very nice steak place and when they took drink orders, I asked to go last. They all ordered a very manly drink so when it came to me, despite really wanting a nice glass of red wine, I ordered and drank the same thing the men drank. I was later told that was a good move on my part because my drink order was what got me voted in. They told me that they worried if a woman could handle their culture and if I drank like a man, I would fit in nicely. I actually felt honored and accepted into a really cool fraternity.

I don't think I have ever been hired as a salesperson that made me feel so important and so appreciated. This entire interview process had me extremely eager to work there. It felt like I was now part of a very elite group of sales professionals and I was thrilled. But the honeymoon didn't last long enough.

Once everybody was hired, we went to corporate and had our first sales meeting. I stood out like a sore thumb because I was the only woman out of about 30 very well dressed and obviously extremely successful sales guys.

The meeting started with a clip from the movie I mentioned in the Preface, *Glengarry Glen Ross*. It was my first exposure to this movie and it made me feel bad for being in sales. For the record, this movie is about every single thing that is wrong with the sales profession and way too many people look to this movie, as the way sales leaders should behave. It's shameful. For those that have never seen or heard about this movie, the clip features a young Alec Baldwin screaming and cussing at a sales team about ABC – Always Be Closing. He also announced a sales contest where the winner would get a new Cadillac, second place would receive kitchen knives, and third place was fired.

Here is a link if you haven't seen it. Over 3.3 million people have viewed this clip – https://www.youtube.com/watch?v=Q4PE2hSqVnk.

The men in the room roared with laughter as they watched the clip. They absolutely loved it. Then the meeting started. In my entire life, I have never heard the F-bomb dropped as much as it was during this meeting. I had never used the F-word so this was very unusual for me. To amuse myself, I started counting all the different ways the word was used. For your information, it is a pretty flexible word. It was used as a Noun, Pronoun, Adverb, Verb, Adjective, and just a stand-alone word. I was now part of a man's club and I was determined to thicken my skin and fit in. I was having fun with this very unusual culture that didn't seem to care about being compliant with HR guidelines. Is this how men behave when women aren't around? I was amused and flattered to be part of this man's world.

This was a team that was extremely competitive and since I was representing all of the women salespeople in the world, I was determined to be at the top of the sales rankings. I worked harder than I have ever worked and had a very healthy pipeline very quickly. It was easy because this product was winning numerous awards and was being talked about in every industry magazine. It was getting media coverage like no other start-up I'd ever seen before. I was sure I was going to be a millionaire on my stocks alone.

I leveraged my very closest client relationships. During one of these efforts, my technical partner told me that he just realized that the product didn't work and that no amount of development would ever make it work. I panicked and I had a hard time wrapping my head around my technical co-worker's claims. This offering had won numerous awards from many publications and analysts! We had customers that were on covers of magazines praising what we were selling. How can it not work if everybody is so positive about it?

Surely my SE was mistaken! So I went directly to someone that I knew would be able to confirm or deny this revelation. He had been drinking when we spoke so he probably told me more than he would have. He explained that he owned a previous company and his software was built on a specific platform and was so new that it had zero clients. Yet a competitor came in and bought his company for over $270 million dollars to keep him out of the game.

He continued explaining that the competitor had no intention of ever using the technology because it was built on a conflicting platform. He taught me that not all companies are purchased because of the quality of the technology; they are purchased because they are a pain and distraction from the various competitor's success. He explained that his company was acquired to kill his company, not to purchase the intellectual property.

His plan was to replicate that same transaction with this company and product. My big take away from this conversation was that it didn't matter that our software didn't work. So once again, what was REALLY for sale, was the company, not our software.

So what about all the poor clients that believed in our marketing message and purchased it? What if they ended up getting fired for buying something that didn't work? It's not our problem is what I was told.

I found another job very quickly and left. I then called and warned my clients so they didn't hurt their careers.

This company did end up being acquired but not for anywhere near the amount the first company went for. Today, the offering is completely dead because the company that acquired the intellectual property was also acquired. My mind is so blow by how much investor money is wasted on things that don't even work!

Lessons Learned – I recommend that you never work for a start- up company until they can produce a client that is truly using the offering and can confirm that it works. I also learned that there is a fine line between brilliant marketing and fraud. It can be incredibly difficult to distinguish between the two.

I once saw a cartoon that showed two salespeople and the caption was "You know what is the difference between a used car salesman and a software salesman?" The answer is, "The used car salesman KNOWS when he is lying."

This is not a funny joke. It is a reality. And it is wrong. My integrity and reputation are the most valuable things I own. Companies like this put everything I've worked my entire life at risk. Beware of companies like this because despite the carrot presented during the interview, you won't be the one to get rich when the company is sold. And don't be naïve; if the company doesn't care about the clients and the careers they are ruining, they won't think twice about hurting you too.

Company #3 –
This was a software company in the energy business and I interviewed here after both of my previous stories so I felt much more confident in my interview skills. I asked to see the list of clients and I was handed a huge list. Great. At least I knew it worked.

I was offered the job and started immediately. On my first day, I asked to see the Master License Agreement. They asked me why and I told them that nobody sells software unless they are selling the intellectual property. What we actually sell, are the licenses and the terms and conditions around the usage of the software. By now, I had been selling software for over 10 years so I knew most negotiations broke down over the terms and conditions in the contract. In the past, I almost lost deals because of the ironclad terms and conditions so I wanted to see how tough their agreements were. My new sales leader looked at me with a blank expression and said he had never seen a contract. Uh oh. This was my first major red flag!

It took a lot of investigating but what I uncovered was that if I sold $100,000 in software, I would only get sales credit and commissions on about $20,000 because most of the intellectual property wasn't even theirs! They had taken another company's software and enhanced it. The reason there wasn't a license agreement was because all new clients had to sign an agreement with the owner of the Intellectual property. They had some basic and simple wording on the purchase order that this company used to cover their usage guidelines. But when you are selling another company's intellectual property, you have zero control over the contract negotiations because it's not your contract to negotiate!

So technically their product DID work. And they DID have clients using it. But it was not a true software company. It was a reseller that created a simple cosmetic enhancement to the interface. That is NOT how they represented their company or their software during the interview process.

Why should I work for them, sell $100,000 worth of software and only get 10% of $20,000 ($2,000) when I could work for the owner of the intellectual property and get 10% ($10,000) of the full amount? Plus, I was used to selling multi-million-dollar transactions and a million-dollar sale was not really a million-dollar sale. I just got a huge pay decrease by accepting this role!

This was just another company that was deceptive during the hiring process and to their clients as well. This is another company I worked for a very short time.

Mentor Tip for Fellow Sales Leaders –
BE HONEST
How can you expect to lead if you deceive?

Lessons Learned –I finally concluded that it would be easier to just work for companies with proven track records and well-known brands than these start-ups that are "faking until they make it." But even big major corporations tend to have offerings that aren't "ready for prime time" yet. So I've made a point to spend time learning what to sell and what NOT to sell at each place I've worked. A lot of salespeople don't do this and clients end up being sold things that don't work (yet).

PROPOSED SOLUTION –

So here is the twist I think needs to be discussed before a true solution can be suggested; I just shared three very different stories of deception. How are they different from what is happening right now with Elizabeth Holmes?

Of the three stories I told you above, only one of those companies is still operating today. Nobody has ever been held accountable for any deceptions.

This book is not about corruption in Corporate America. This is about how the corruption in Corporate America affects the image of salespeople. If we are going to change things, we have to start holding EVERYBODY accountable for deception. Why do some people get embarrassing articles written about them yet their careers are unscathed and others go on trial and prison for doing the exact same thing?

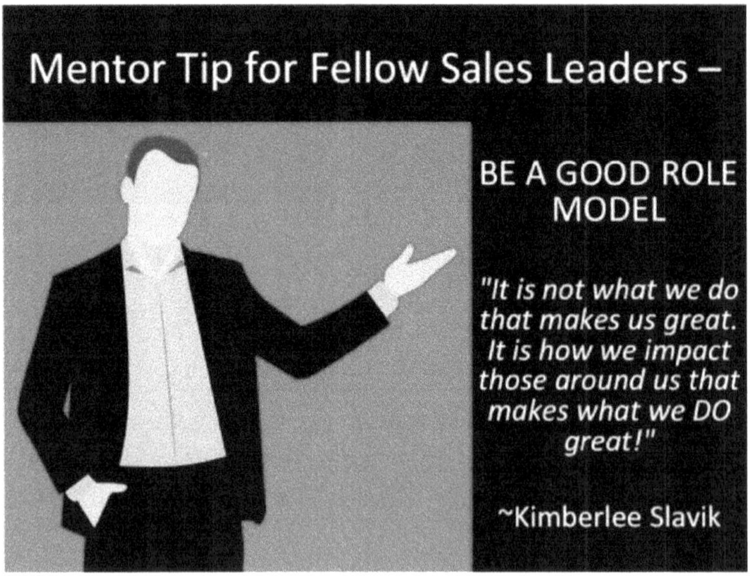

Mentor Tip for Fellow Sales Leaders –
BE A GOOD ROLE MODEL
"It is not what we do that makes us great. It is how we impact those around us that makes what we DO great!"
~Kimberlee Slavik

Once leaders at the very top are held accountable for deception, they may be less likely to support deceptive marketing collateral that turns innocent sales professionals into liars. The important word in this sentence is "may."

Until this happens, "Buyers Beware" is VERY applicable to every single salesperson interviewing for jobs today. Give us something real to sell and make sure what we are selling is worthy of our efforts.

Be careful not to judge salespeople negatively for leaving companies quickly. The stories I have shared in this book have never been mentioned during interviews. Nor SHOULD they be mentioned! However, when a salesperson leaves a company, it's automatically assumed something is wrong with the salesperson. How many really great talented people are overlooked because of their job tenures on resumes? I know that many recruiters have told me that their clients won't interview me because of my "job hopping."

How many ethical and successful sales pros have been filed in the round filing cabinet (trash) before they were given a proper assessment? A good sales leader will focus on RESULTS listed on a resume versus tenure. Especially today with Millennials and Generation Z's in the workplace, sales leaders better get used to job-hopping. Finding successful salespeople is going to get more difficult but KEEPING good salespeople is going be almost impossible without exceptional sales leadership.

Inspirational Quote -

"Leadership is an obligation and you need to step up every day."

~Vince Molinaro

And as we have already started discussing, most companies don't have strong leadership. Why is that? Here are some things to consider improving. We have already started to identify many of these topics in the first few chapters of this book;

1. On boarding process for ALL sales roles MUST be improved!
2. Where is the training for LEADERSHIP?
3. How can companies make each new hire feel special?
4. What type of career path has your company developed to show a progression in each sales role (not just each sales PERSON) career path? Today, if young professionals don't receive promotions and new challenges, they will leave.
5. Instead of the silly perks today of free food, why not get back to offering tuition reimbursement? My employers paid for my business degree. But once I got my degree, I left for a better job. I've been told that this is why most companies stopped tuition reimbursement programs. Why not include an employment contract? I think these programs are worth taking a second look at because the magnitude of student loans today is mind blowing.

I will cover additional sales leadership suggestions as you continue reading.

CHAPTER 3 –

Compensation Drives Behavior – Be Careful You Are Not Incenting Good People to Do Bad Things.

Mentor Tip for Fellow Sales Leaders –
INCENT AND REWARD WELL
"Compensation Drives Behavior."
~Kimberlee Slavik

When we hear the word, "Compensation," we tend to think of salary, bonuses, commissions, benefits, and other monetary rewards. However, compensation can also be tied to employee reviews. These reviews can impact career paths, morale, motivation, loyalty, trust, and of course, bonuses and salary increases. I could write an entire book on this chapter alone but most of what I want to say would be common sense and nothing surprising.

This book is intended to shock the reader (especially LEADERSHIP) into seeing things that are currently invisible to them. It's important to acknowledge that many casual decisions not only cause people to leave because they hate their jobs, those decisions also impede sales results. In other words, an abusive sales culture will cost way more money than you are trying to save!

PROBLEM IDENTIFIED – Performance Reviews and Sales Reports focus too much on just sales closures and pipelines.

Let's start by considering the employee performance review. Salespeople are the primary employees whose performance statuses are constantly exposed thanks, in part, to the documentation and tracking of sales numbers. However, revenue generation is not the only way sales success should be measured.

Early in my career I worked at a start-up when dot-coms were going bust at an alarming rate. Because I knew that selling is a numbers game, I was extremely disciplined in making between 50 and 100 calls each day setting appointments. But I struggled closing opportunities because clients were hesitant to risk their careers buying from a company that could go under any day. The result was that I WENT AN ENTIRE YEAR WITH ZERO CLOSES!

Thankfully, I had one of the best sales leaders in my career. His name was Gary and each morning, he called me to lift me up, remind me to keep doing the right things and reassuring me that the results would come. He worked very hard to keep me from resigning. Not once, did he ever beat me up or make me question my abilities! How unusual is THAT from a Sales Leader in today's world of reports and documentation?!

Fast-forward a year after I started. My beloved Sales Manager, Gary, was demoted due to our low sales, our start-up was acquired by a huge corporation, and suddenly all those scared potential clients felt comfortable investing in my software.

I had record-breaking sales for the next three years and was the #1 Salesperson GLOBALLY all three of those years. In fact, two of those years, I was the only one in the entire sales organization to hit my quota numbers and I was shattering them. What was the difference between me and the other salespeople? Most of them were brand new in their roles, they were building new client relationships, and they had to build brand new pipelines. I, on the other hand, had been planting those seeds for over a year and it was my time to harvest. I basically had a year head start on the new people. I was the only original salesperson that hung in there during the tough times. Most left when our beloved Gary was demoted. None of us thought he was treated fairly given the attitudes towards dot-coms and those circumstances in which he was leading us. He was a GREAT leader! But the Execs in the company demoted him because they were completely out of touch with the challenges the sales team faced. Needless to say, none of them ever went on a sales call with me or anybody else for that matter.

With this type of disconnect, sales leaders can't survive with just one person achieving her sales quota; so I went through SEVEN VPs of Sales in just FIVE years. Each time one was fired, I was approached to take the vacant VP Role. Why in the world would I want to do that? I made a LOT more money than my VPs, my job was much more secure, they worked way more hours than I did, had to attend a ton of goofy meetings, and why would I want to put my family's financial well-being in jeopardy because of other people's incompetence?! I actually had to fight to stay an Individual Contributor because the company knew they could pay me less if they could talk me into taking a Vice President title.

For the record, at this stage of my career, I would have been a terrible sales leader. I was way too self-absorbed. In fact, I haven't seen many people successfully transition from a successful salesperson to a sales leader. They are two very different roles and just because someone can sell well, it doesn't mean they will be a good leader. Most of them will need a LOT of training before they are anywhere close to being competent in a leadership role. It's tough to change your competitive attitude towards your peers or that top spot, to suddenly wanting to help them beat the sales records YOU set as a salesperson.

Even back then, it was obvious to me that senior executives expected the new sales leaders to change things up quickly. (Aka - fire the new people that hadn't closed business yet.) The only thing that the executives from the acquiring company knew about the new sales team they purchased, was that one salesperson was blowing away her numbers and all the others were not selling anything. They had just acquired our company so they had no idea how long I had been there and how new these other people were. I witnessed a lot of poor staffing decisions being made. I didn't want to be part of that leadership style. I just wanted to do my job and make a ton of cash. The turnover was sad; I watched this cost the company sales.

Based upon how quickly new salespeople were terminated, had any of Gary's replacements been my manager during my first year, I would have also been terminated and many of my opportunities would not have closed. Terminating salespeople before they complete a full year is one of the biggest mistakes I see happening at every single sized company for which I have worked.

And each time I closed a deal, I watched these short-term sales leaders get pats on the backs for my accomplishments when in reality, the one leader that truly deserved the kudos was the man that was demoted. Had it not been for Gary's patience and motivation, I would have given up and very few of the deals in my pipeline would have closed by my replacement because most of my pipeline were clients that I had sold to in the past.

Here is a major fact that most sales leadership at all levels seems to ignore – **TURNOVER COSTS A LOT OF MONEY!** Most of those balls that were in the air by the salespeople that left will get dropped because their replacements are drinking from a fire hose. Plus, if you think everything is being put into your database, you are sadly mistaken. Furthermore, clients tend to get uncomfortable when someone they like and trust leaves a company. Clients often feel betrayed and are reluctant to invest more time in someone that they believe probably won't last any longer than the last Sales Representative.

PROPOSED SOLUTION –

Executives need to stop believing that forecasting tools hold all the answers for their decision-making. The reality is that they only tell part of the story. Leadership at ALL levels needs to get more engaged with the frontline salespeople. Bad decisions are being made based upon partial data from reports. The only way to really know what is going on, is to get involved in the actions taking place at the field level.

Executives must get involved with their clients versus their beloved CRM (Incorrectly called a Customer Relationship Management when they are really being used as a Customer SALES Management) Tool. And executives, stockholders, and investors need to have patience because sales rarely happen overnight. Relationships and trust grow stronger over time. Turnover is costing more than they realize because these things will not show up in a CRM report.

Also, for the first year of a salesperson's career, let them know you are committed to them for their entire first year. Don't allow the "noise" to start in their heads or allow them to feel insecure. Offer them an MBO (Management by Objective) incentive package for the first six months versus a non-recoverable draw. Give them clear objectives that are realistic and attainable that will help encourage them to plant those seeds.

PROBLEM IDENTIFIED - Executives may be shocked at the lying and cheating going on by people that are "working their plans." Many plans are NOT driving the right types of behaviors.

The story I am about to share with you is one of the most painful stories I will tell you because it destroyed a young man's image of sales forever. Which means, it has impacted his respect and image of his own Mother.

During his senior year in college, a woman took her son on a Quota Attainment Club Trip to Hawaii. He was impressed by the concerts and food and awards ceremonies. He loved the hotel room and the free toys and the special way they were treated. The son had never been with his mother on a trip because she had always brought her husband. However, he was busy with work and the trip fell between semesters so it was perfect timing for some quality Mother/Son time. They had a blast! It was during this trip that the son decided that he wanted to do this for a living so he went through the interview process and was hired (without the Mother's help) into a very elite program of college graduates.

Most of you reading this know that college graduates entering the world of sales are typically hired as Inside Sales Reps. The objective of the inside sales role is to set meetings for the more experienced Field Sales Reps. Most of you reading also know that this is the most painful sales role and requires many calls and constant rejection.

The son won numerous awards during his sales training. His confidence was at an all-time high. However, after a few months in his new role, his self-esteem took a beating and his morale decline rapidly. The Mother kept reassuring him that this was sort of a "hazing" process in his career and it would be temporary and worth it in a few years. The Mother also chalked it up to the millennial generation's unfamiliarity with rejection so she even found it a little amusing to watch her son struggle with success for the first time in his very new career.

However, one day, the son called her and he was very stern and asked, "Mom, did you lie and cheat to win that trip to Hawaii?" The Mother was stunned and said, "Of course not! Why would you dare ask me that?!"

As inside salespeople, their roles were to set meetings. The son was accustomed to being a top performer so when the team rankings were posted and he saw his name at the bottom of the performers, it greatly concerned him. So he went to management to ask for additional coaching. They put him with a young man that was hired the previous year and did so well that he was quickly promoted into a leadership role. The son was thrilled to have this successful peer teach him how to be better at setting appointments.

The young man began by explaining that if he wanted to survive the company culture, he had to "play the game." He taught the son to leverage LinkedIn to look up executives in his assigned territory and to read their profiles. Then he told the son to search their names online and read as much as he could about the contact and try and find out what is important to them. Great advice. Right? Hold on. You are not going to believe what happened next.

He then demonstrated to the son how to lie in the CRM system. He told him that everybody at the top of the rankings was doing exactly what he was teaching him to do.

He told the son to fill out some sort of meeting acceptance form and document as many details as possible from his research to ensure that it looked like he had actually talked with the potential client. Then he instructed the son to just pick a date and time and say that the client agreed to meet to learn more about the company offerings.

Next, he proceeded to teach the son how to setup a web conference and invite the Field Sales Representative and the pre-sales technical support people to attend the fake meeting. He told the son that these valuable tips he was sharing would make the meeting seem legitimate. Furthermore, since their quota was based on the number of meetings that were **scheduled**, he would get credit for this meeting even though the client would never show up!

The son questioned if people would get mad at him for wasting resources and time. The response was that hardly any clients ever showed up for the "real" meetings anyway so nobody ever got mad or shocked when clients didn't join the call. This young mentor continued explaining that "Nobody will suspect a thing and if you do five of these a day, you will be at the top of the ranking chart very quickly. I got promoted to management for doing this!"

After the Mother listened to all the details of this scam, she asked him to imagine it is five years in the future and now her son was in a leadership role and this young man that gave him this advice was looking for a job. The Mother asked her son if he would hire his mentor. The response was a resounding NO! She asked why and the answer was that this guy was a liar and a cheat. She explained that this young manager might think he is winning right now but he has actually destroyed his "brand" and his reputation FOREVER. The Mother also told her son that while it may seem like this cheating and lying is effective, it will catch up to all of them one day and these tactics along with their bad reputations will follow them throughout their careers. The son was wise to point out that there isn't anybody to report this behavior to because he suspected several levels of management were all in on it.

In this life, and especially in business, you will be faced with situations every single day that threaten your reputation and integrity. When you come against one that you aren't sure what to do, always ask yourself, "at the end of this life, will I be judged on the worldly results of this decision (i.e. commissions and/or rankings) or will I be judged on how I handled this decision despite the fall out or ramifications (i.e. doing the honest thing and losing commissions)?"

In this life, people will have the power to take away your home, your job, your car, etc. but nobody can ever take away your reputation or your "brand' so guard that carefully because it's the one thing you leave behind in this world that really matters.

Be careful with whom you surround yourself because "If you go into a bar, you will come out smelling like a smoker." In other words, your environment DOES affect you. The culture you choose to surround yourself could potentially put you at risk of absorbing some of those traits and/or becoming confused about what is right and wrong. So choose your friends and co-workers carefully. Surround yourself with people you respect and admire and strive each day to be worthy of them reciprocating the same opinion of you.

The point of this story is that many good people have had their innocence and optimism shattered by a compensation plan that was driving horrific behaviors. And MANAGEMENT is often in on it.

Both Mother and Son resigned from this company within a few weeks of each other. Good people leave environments like this and companies are left with the liars and cheaters. And sadly, these people become leaders and the culture becomes more and more corrupted.

PROPOSED SOLUTION –

The key message in this story is that compensation is driving behaviors like this. If it is true that several levels of management are aware of this cheating, chances are high that their compensation and quotas are also tied to the same requirements. Re-evaluate what you consider to be acceptable results. Do you really want meetings SET or do you really want meetings HELD?

Evaluate each layer of leadership's incentive plans. It's not a good idea to have several layers incented for the same results. Perhaps the inside sales team can be compensated for the number of meetings set. But their managers should be measured by the percentage of meetings that actually occurred. This would keep the individual contributors from being encouraged by leadership to cheat. And it would incent leadership to ensure no "fake meetings" took place that would negatively impact their "meetings held" quota.

One of the comments that really stood out to me in this story is that "even REAL meetings" rarely happen. So if you want the RESULT to be that more meetings actually take place, why not drive that behavior? Are your salespeople properly following up with reminders? I find that email reminders are not productive and people are much more responsive to texts. Are your sales teams incented to try and get cell numbers? I'm just brain storming here. I'd love readers to send me their ideas and suggestions and I can share their ideas in future releases.

As I shared the draft of this book, one of the readers of Visnostic Selling shared this idea – ***"My current hypothesis is that the key to getting the prospect into the appointment is really having documented what is important to THEM (I call it WITT), and use that as the driving force (words said). When reminding them of the meeting, the emphasis in words is not the meeting but instead reminding them of what is important to them (the WITT)."*** And this is exactly what Visnostic Statements do!

A woman I admire owns a company that specializes in setting

appointments. Her company is called "BlitzMasters" and the results from her training are remarkable. Invest in specific skillset training so your team can set meetings that are legit. BTW, when you combine her training with the Visnostic approach I teach, the results are mind blowing!

Be sure to determine what specific actions are effective and compensate accordingly. This is another great example of how an external and temporary sales leadership team can make a huge impact. Who within your company came up with the original sales objectives? Someone needs to educate that person on what the actual outcome was.

This is also a great example why internal advisory boards are so important. I was invited to be on an advisory board because I was a top performer. Having top performers participate on an advisory board is a logical decision. But why not also include representatives on the board that are underperforming? They will have a completely different perspective than the overachievers. Think about if the son had been invited to be on an advisory board, what could have been uncovered! Instead, he quietly left without telling anybody why he became so disillusioned. How many other GOOD and LEGITIMATE employees left? How much does attrition cost? Is this tracked? It should be!

In fact, I've often wished that I had been given better exit interviews. The reason this book is so difficult to write is because I have been taught to never burn a bridge, never talk bad about your previous employers, and don't get labeled a complainer. Besides, I'm a Southern Girl and it's extremely rude to leave a company in a negative way. So every exit interview I have ever been given, I was extremely complimentary to the company and my leadership. I would never want to say anything to get anybody fired or hurt someone's career in anyway. But what if you PAY people to give you constructive feedback? That changes everything!

PAY people that leave for giving constructive feedback about anything they viewed as broken. Even if I left angry, if I received a call from HR offering to PAY me just to speak with them, I might consider this offer! If they assured me that I could be completely honest without retaliation, that my feedback would be taken in a constructive manner, and that I would get paid based upon the value of my input, I would be all over that! How innovative is THAT?! I sincerely believe the lack of respect for sales in general and the disposable attitude about firing salespeople is why this approach isn't already happening.

I am an optimistic person and I would think by now, someone has realized that hardly any meetings are occurring. I also assume someone eventually started expressing concern over how much time and salaries were being wasted prepping and attending the fake meetings. I also realize that this example is not applicable to many of the readers. But how does this example translate to your world? What weaknesses exist in your current compensation plan? How do you trust your own people to know what needs to change? I highly recommend bringing in someone from the outside to assess things from a non-political perspective. Third parties often speak to hundreds of companies so chances are high that they have ideas your team has not considered. And there are no agendas or fears with a 3rd party.

If you can't see that this is costing the company money, you should just put this book down right now because nothing else I write about will resonate with you. I'm writing this book to wake people up. These are stories that I believe and hope senior executives are oblivious to. I believe that Execs are too comfortable in their corporate jets and multi-million-dollar salaries to take time to get to know what is really going on in their companies.

Sales can be an honorable profession but it MUST start at the very top to ensure this happens.

However, salespeople have a responsibility as well. Unfortunately, in today's world, more emphasis is placed upon winning than honor and integrity. Somehow, these lessons are not being taught at home like they were several generations ago. When salespeople see a compensation plan that is driving the wrong behavior, they should feel comfortable letting leadership know immediately! How about a reward system that pays for any information about unethical behaviors?

Mentor Tip for Fellow Sales Pros –
"Your Behavior Can Make Sales A More Respected Profession! ."
~ Kimberlee Slavik, Author of Memoirs of An Angry Sales Pro – Sales Leadership MUST change!

Everybody's behavior, at every level in a sales organization, impacts the image of the sales profession. While Sales leadership MUST change, so should the attitudes and behaviors of the salespeople. If something feels wrong, it probably IS wrong. Don't be like the young man that cheated to get a promotion. Don't blow your future by making bad decisions TODAY.

YOUR behavior can make sales a more respected profession! And your behavior can also perpetuate the already bad stereotype of selling.

Be what is GOOD about sales, don't be what is BAD about sales! It WILL catch up with you some day.

PROBLEM IDENTIFIED –
Many performance reviews are actually causing chaos and are driving destructive behaviors.

As your sales manager, HR wants me to give you performance reviews. I have more important things to do so I will just criticize you in public occasionally instead.

I wrote the following article in 2012 and posted it as a note on Facebook. People from this company actually de-friended me over this post. So please note that the details have been edited to avoid any additional retribution.

The Demise of One of America's Greatest Corporate Stories - October 4, 2012 at 10:45 AM
(The Company Founders) must be spinning in their respective graves right now watching their beloved company destroyed by dysfunction, greed, and incompetent leadership. Let me take a few minutes and explain why a company with stock prices around $52/share in 2011 is now plummeting today and are currently around $14/share and positioned for a takeover, acquisition, or sell-off.

As a new manager, I came in and was explained how to rank my team. There were three rankings (A, C, & Z). An "A" was a superstar. You didn't have to identify an "A" person on your team but you could have no more than ONE person on your team that was an "A." A "Z" person was an under achiever. This is someone that would be targeted if and when WFRs (Work Force Reduction) or RIFs (Reductions In Force) were necessary. You could have as many "Z's" on your team as you wanted. But you HAD to have at least ONE. If an employee was not a "Z" and not an "A" then they got a "C" rating.

Let me explain why this sets a company up for failure;

1. *If all managers know they MUST have a "Z" on their team, management will no longer try and help their people succeed. If someone if failing, it's easier to just sit back and watch him or her fail because it will make the manager's job that much easier when it's time to conduct performance reviews.*
2. *If a struggling employee reaches out to his/her teammates for help or support, it's highly unlikely the employee will receive help because the reality is that under these rules; the team WANTS to see someone fail. When a teammate fails, it takes the pressure off the others from getting the dreaded "Z" rating. So this rule puts every team in competition with each other - not to WIN - but competing not to FAIL. Therefore,*

there can never be a true team.

3. *When people got "A" ratings, it was kept a very big secret because if word got out which team member was an "A," jealousy amongst the group developed because "A" employees received a huge bonus and stocks. Again, nobody on a team wants to help each other because they are also competing for the top ranking. And nobody wants people on their team to know they got an "A" because they feared jealousy and retribution.*
4. *I've never seen so many butt-kissers in my entire career. Everybody wanted their manager to like them. As a leader, I inherited a team full of fake people that I didn't trust.*
5. *Because of the fear of becoming a Z, there was a lot of negative information hidden from leadership and a lot of cover-ups going on.*
6. *When I left this company, I actually had three different recruiters tell me that having this company on my resume was hurting their ability to help me find a job. It was known in the marketplace that people coming from this culture were not go-getters or top performers.*
7. *The "A" rating tended to be a rotating benefit versus a deserved designation. I attended management meetings where this was actually openly discussed. Managers wanted to be "fair" by giving each member of their team a chance at this rating. So it was a rotating designation versus a deserved reward for exceptional performance.*
8. *As a leader, my instinct is to have a team of over achievers. Unfortunately this rating system extinguished this objective. When people on a team fail, leadership should be accountable. This is not applicable with this rating system.*
9. *And Butt-kissing was rewarded! During the 4 years I was at this company, I'd never seen so many incompetent people promoted and rewarded because they were incredible POLITICIANS vs. innovative thinkers or team players.*

The result of this silly system is a management team that doesn't care about its people. It creates paranoia, backstabbing, distrust, political positioning, distractions, contempt and lethargic behaviors (better to "fly under the radar" and be a "C" than a "Z" or "A"). In other words, it creates a toxic work environment that promotes bad behaviors at all levels. It destroys innovative thinking to its core.

When I worked with one of this company's competitors, I recall during our competitive training "Never worry about competing with (this company) because the GOOD people leave and the BAD people are not a threat." With a system like this, I can see why GOOD people leave - they know this is wrong and this type of system will never allow them to be the best they can be. And I can see why BAD people stay - they are beaten down, defeated, and lose the confidence to pursue other options. Many of these people don't know any other way. I can also see why companies would NOT want to hire people from this company. These employees are victims of their own toxic environment and eventually behave like an abused dog that trusts no one.

Ironically, I recall studying this company in Business School. We learned how it grew into a powerhouse of technology. Sadly, I predict future students will be studying its demise and students will be taught what NOT to do. I hope this insane performance review process is part of the "what NOT to do" that is studied!

This is just one of many examples of how a company, once known for innovation and invention, is now in a situation of vulnerability for a hostile takeover. Today, it is a "me too" company with weak management that focuses on what people LOOK like more than how they PERFORM.

(End of 2012 article)

Surely performance review rules like these are created by people that have never been a decent leader, never wanted to help their employees succeed, and/or have no clue how to motivate people to do their best! And I've been on BOTH sides of this ridiculous quota system!

During my last review, although I exceeded every objective I was given at the beginning of the year, I received a C- rating. Needless to say, I took issue with this rating. Not only did I exceed my goals, I completed all of my major projects way ahead of schedule and won numerous awards and various bonuses and recognition throughout the year. Furthermore, I didn't receive one bit of criticism during the entire year. Nor did I receive any constructive criticism during my review. So when I met face-to-face with my VP (over 20 years at the company) and challenged him on my ranking/review, this is what he said to me, "Come on Kim. You are a people manager. You know how this game is played. I have a quota. This year you got the short straw. Next year, you will probably get a better ranking. I don't know why you care anyway. You didn't get a "Z" so your job is safe."

It was at this moment that I checked out because one thing was crystal clear to me – he didn't respect my work or contributions and his ranking decisions were a popularity contest to him and I could tell exactly how little he cared about what I thought about him and the situation. This was my CAREER he so casually impacted. I started interviewing that afternoon. As the previous employer had taught us during competitive training – the GOOD ones won't tolerate this treatment/culture so they will leave and the ones that stay, aren't a threat. And worse yet, leaders are trained to perpetuate this bad behavior.

This VP was one of the beloved "Lifers" and he stayed until he retired. He is actually a really nice person but he is also a product of a bad culture and since this was his only job for his entire career, he couldn't possibly know how wrong it was. It was all he knew so this was his normal. These types of leaders that stay around never question authority because they have been conditioned not to care. They are all politicians FIRST. They just follow orders and "manage above them." How can a company ever get better with this type of leadership in place?

That is just ONE of many stories I have around how this performance review was impacting the company in a negative way.

One of the first things I did with my new team when I came on board was to hold an onsite meeting at our headquarters to discuss the performance plan. I also should note that when I was hired, I was told upfront that there were three people on my team that needed to be terminated. I requested that names not be shared with me because I wanted to fairly assess the team. It didn't take long to discover that my team was a bunch of politicians. I wanted to make sure it was clear to each of them that their reviews would not be a popularity contest. I continued by explaining the reason we were meeting was to determine measurable goals that were non-subjective so that everybody was measured fairly and equally. We agreed on a ranking system based upon denominators such as YoY (Year over Year) growth each month. I made it crystal clear that no amount of butt kissing would change these rankings or cause any debates.

Our year was off to a great start and each of the members of my new team understood and agreed with the way they were being measured. There were no surprises when each person saw his ranking. One of the men on my team was outstanding. He requested a standing meeting once a week at 6am to go over his business plan and how he was tracking. This initiative contributed to his #1 ranking on the team. He was the only member to hit his numbers every quarter so he was doing an excellent job and nobody could accuse me of favoritism; the revenue numbers told the story of who my top performer was.

Unfortunately, there was a reorg and my hiring manager was moved and a new VP was brought in from a very aggressive competitor. In fact, he came from one of those companies that I declined invitations to interview because the company reputation was so poor. It's also one of those companies that did great (short term) but today, it no longer exists!

And one of the first things this new VP did was to tell me that he wanted me to give my #1 manager a poor review (a "Z" ranking) so we could terminate him. I pushed back and said the entire team knows he is the #1 performer on the team. I was told this was an order not a request. I asked why and the response was that he had a buddy he wanted to hire.

I said that I didn't feel comfortable with his request because this would impact my integrity and the momentum I was building with my "results-based" management style. He clarified that this was not a request, it was an order. He then threatened me with my own review and told me he would give ME the "Z" instead of the guy he wanted terminated if I didn't comply.

I told him to do what he needed to do but I couldn't justify a bad review for someone that had been doing an outstanding job.

The result was that I got a "Z" and he called me insubordinate during my review and actually put that in writing for my permanent HR file. While I didn't get terminated because my results were too good, I did get moved out of a very powerful leadership role, into an Individual contributor role.

The good news is that I no longer reported to this new VP.

Inspirational Quote –
Some of the best advice I have been given:

"Don't take criticism from people you would never go to for advice."

I ran into him a few months later at a conference and he asked me to join him for dinner. He had such an annoying smirk on his face as he asked me if I regretted not obeying him and I said, "At the end of this life, I won't be judged on what rating you gave me on my performance review but I WILL be judged on how I handled the situation you put me in and I don't regret my decision at all." He then stood up, angrily pushed his chair into the table and said, "This is why women shouldn't be in leadership roles! They can't make difficult business decisions!"

Excuse me?!

Actually, I DID make a difficult business decision and I stand by it! In fact, it's one of my proudest decisions because it was the RIGHT thing to do despite the personal damage that was done to my career. I put ethics above politics. And I put my team above myself.

Why did I share all these details? **Performance Reviews should NEVER be used as a power play, blackmail, punishment, or for political gain.** As you read this story, I hope you reflect on your own performance review process and work with your HR team to ensure no manager or employee is bullied or threatened in the way I just described. In case you wondered what happened to my #1 manager that I was told to fire: I told him I was being forced out and I told him why. I was a reference for him and he left the company and has been wildly successful in his new role and with his new company. He has been there for over ten years now and is in leadership! On the other hand, the VP did bring in his buddy and he was NOT as successful as my #1 manager. What did it cost the company for these political maneuvers to be allowed? Good people will leave due to these unethical and political tactics. Yet this VP stayed in his role way too long destroying great people's careers along the way. It cost a LOT!!!

Since I originally wrote this article, current leaders have told me that this ranking system has been modified greatly. However, major damage has been done and it will take years to repair. The core of the culture has been impacted by this silly system of reviewing performance. I work with people from this company today and I can see that the innovation is gone. The "me-too" attitude is prevalent in their offerings. I see the company chasing the competition instead of threatening the competition. And although I am currently working hard to help with their messaging, I am constantly blocked to bring in my innovative approach because "it's too new." What happened to the innovative culture that the founders worked so hard to build?

PROPOSED SOLUTION –

There really needs to be some sort of checks and balances for all performance appraisals. While I was given the opportunity to respond to my review, and I DID, nobody seemed to care. This was normal business practice and the entire point of the appraisal process was to figure out who would be on the chopping block and who would get stocks and bonuses. If this is what performance appraisals are for, why bother ranking and reviewing the "C" people at all? Why not just speak with the Top and Lowest performers? What a waste of time and resources to do things this way. How demotivating! As a leader, I spent an entire month every single year doing these silly performance reviews. What a waste of valuable sales time!

Make sure that NON-SUBJECTIVE expectations are clearly defined before each appraisal year begins. Make sure all requirements are measurable. Eliminate as many opportunities to provide subjective feedback. Subjective commentary is almost always impacted by politics and personal agendas and leaves employees feeling betrayed and unfairly treated.

Bring in 3rd parties to review your current appraisal process and give unbiased feedback. DynaExec was created for this exact reason. Fractional Sales Leadership should be a norm in every company because leveraging the experience of a company that isn't on the payroll will allow perspectives to be shared that the internal politics will never allow.

Employees won't want to tell the Emperor that he is naked because they may receive a "Z" rating and lose their jobs. Fractional Sales Leaders are motivated to do the exact opposite of this. This is a very unique and interesting issue caused by the **ENC Syndrome**.

Many Executives have lost touch at the field level. I understand that they don't have the bandwidth to be at every customer meeting but relying on mid-managers to report the truth to them is naïve. In fact, all levels of leadership will be reluctant to reveal anything that may be a poor reflection on their own performance. In other cases, they may be too incompetent or inexperienced to be able to identify areas of improvement needed. And lastly, I've been a mid-level sale leader for over 15 years. The number of meetings and reports expected from this level of leadership is absurd. There are very few hours left for leaders to do what they were hired to do, which is to properly lead sales organizations. **This has to change!**

I was an individual contributor and worked for a company early in my career that had the absolute best executive team I have ever seen. During an Achievement Club Trip, the CEO and CMO approached me together to personally invite me to become part of their advisory panel. They even explained that because I was the number one sales rep, they wanted to eliminate the layers of management between us, and they wanted to hear the good, the bad, and the ugly from me directly so they didn't lose touch with reality.

They knew that by the time my message would get to them, it would be watered down, edited, and politicized by several layers of managers. Do YOU have an advisory panel of first line employees? Why not? Do you honestly think their full message is making its way up the food chain by their own managers? If you answered yes, I advise you to take a closer look by spending time with the salespeople and their clients. I bet you will be shocked at what is really going on and what is not being reported to you.

PROBLEM IDENTIFIED –
Quota Club Trips ARE important but difficult to get right. Most Leaders attempt to establish a universal approach with each employee. This is impossible and especially with salespeople because every person is different.

I LOVE Sales Quota Trips! I get excited to get those days off without having to dip into my vacation days. I appreciate all the planning that goes into those trips. With the exception of one club trip to Phoenix, I always leave those trips fired up and motivated to earn the next one! 99% of the time, I come back extremely motivated and fired up to sell more than I did the previous year! I LOVE meeting top performers from all over the world and picking their brains and getting new ideas how I can become an even better sales professional!

However, I've worked with people that absolutely hated the thought of being with their co-workers outside of work. They complained about paying taxes on a trip that they didn't even want. They would prefer to take a cash equivalent instead of being forced on a trip with people that they don't necessarily even like. And they complain about the destinations. After all, how many times can a person enjoy Hawaii? I don't understand these people but I respect that they have different motivations than I do. As a Sales Leader, I worked very hard to get to know the members of my team so I knew what was important to them and why.

Most Salespeople are profiled as people that love to golf and drink and play with clients all day. Therefore, many club trips are geared towards this type of salesperson. I've been to club trips in Palm Springs, Palm Beach, Carmel, and the Phoenician. These were my least favorite trips because they were domestic and very focused on golfing. I know how to golf but I don't have the patience to be really be good at it. I enjoy driving the golf cart and I enjoy exploring the gorgeous courses more than the actual game. But I've worked with people that live and breathe for these types of club trips. It's fascinating to me how difficult it is to find something that is universally appealing to an entire sales organization. Sometimes it is pretty obvious that the trips are actually geared towards the Executive Team and what THEY want to do versus what the sales teams want to do.

During a sales kick off meeting, our VP of Sales had a photo of the car that was in the latest James Bond movie. It was a BMW convertible two-seater. It was so beautiful and sexy. He had my attention! I was feeling burned out and the new sales year had just started so my numbers were back to zero after blowing away my previous years' quota. I even won Rookie of the Year out of hundreds of new hires worldwide so I had a lot to be proud of. But my attitude was not good because our club trip was in Phoenix. I didn't like golf so I spent the days at the spa. I was bored and I was disappointed in the club trip destination. But now I was seeing a brand-new sexy car being projected during our sales meeting so our VP had my full attention. Could we each win that car or will just one of us win it?? He went on and on about the engine and the color of the car and how gorgeous it was and I was totally sold! How do I earn it?! Tell me how much I have to sell to get that car! Then he dropped the bombshell that even today boggles my mind. He said that if each of us hit our new quotas, he would make "X" amount of money in bonuses and would be paying cash to buy that car for HIMSELF. And that when each of us hit our respective quotas, he would let us BORROW the car for a full weekend!

What?! THAT is supposed to motivate me? We are going to help YOU buy YOURSELF a new car and we get to BORROW it for a weekend when we hit our numbers? I wasn't the only one that was deflated after hearing the actual motivation he was waving in front of us. But one thing was crystal clear – he was completely out of touch with what was important to his team and had no clue how to properly motivate us.

I have worked for companies that didn't even have an achievement club. The attitude there is that salespeople should be motivated to sell in order to keep their jobs and to make the commission. WRONG. This screams a culture that believes "Sales is a necessary evil." A guy that reported to me actually told me that he didn't care if he hit his numbers or not because the more he made, the more went to his ex-wife's child support. He preferred trips because she can't count that as income.

PROPOSED SOLUTION–

Know your team and find out what is important to each of them individually.

When I was in my 20's, our company had a little baby boom and many of the top performers had young children. I have to give huge kudos to that leadership team because once they saw the names on the trip awards, they quickly identified the majority were young families and the decision was made to make it a club trip to Disney World. To this day, this was my very favorite club trip. The Golfers got to golf and the families got to enjoy Disney World. At night, we all met at the clubs and childcare was provided. That was a club trip that I do not recall one single complaint. However, it wouldn't be as appealing to me today because of where I am in my life so what a great assessment and decision by the Executive Team.

If you have a diverse team, why not consider awards that are customizable for each person's particular motivation? Perhaps awarding a travel voucher and add extra vacation days to their vacation pool would be appreciated.

But you must have something extra to incent salespeople to hit those numbers. Everybody knows that they make commission when they sell. But how will their life change if they actually hit quota? There has to be more incentive than making those commissions. Give them a reason to be angry with themselves if they miss quota by $1! If you are relying on sales to be happy with their commissions, think about what I just said. If you don't have an achievement club and a salesperson missed quota by $1, why would they care? Chances are you pay them 10% so they lost 10 cents. But if it was a $10,000 travel voucher and three extra vacation days, they are going to be upset! Don't let them view quota as a "suggestion." Make them see that making quota gets them commission AND a special reward.

Another incentive is that once they hit quota, their commissions should have accelerators. So instead of 10% commission, it jumps to 15% for all sales over quota. But don't do this instead of the Quota Club incentive. Do it IN ADDITION to the Quota Club incentive.

If you are reading this and are shaking your head because you'd rather not pay out thousands of extra dollars, you have a bigger problem than you are admitting. You do not want to be the culture of “Sales is a necessary evil.” Your salespeople will feel it and they will not stay. And guess what? Your competitors have club trips. Which company do you think top talent will prefer to work?

Ok. So maybe this claim is bit of a stretch. So let’s say that in your particular industry, nobody does club trips. Wouldn’t you LOVE for the top producers at your competitors to beg to work for YOU?!

Trust me when I say that not having that extra incentive IS costing you more than the actual incentive amount!

CHAPTER 4 – Pay Us Well and Give Us Realistic and Attainable Goals!

The most common questions asked by candidates during a sales interview are:

- "What is the compensation package?"
- "What is the quota?
- "What is the OTE (On Target Earning)?"

Once again, I could write an entire book on this topic but I'm going to keep this short and sweet.

PROBLEMS IDENTIFIED –
Capped commission plans are the dumbest thing ever invented.

I debated if I should even bring up this topic but it exists and if it wakes up even one Reader, it is important.

A competitor that I had just beat reached out to me because they wanted to hire me. They were very aggressive so I accepted a meeting. During this meeting, I was told that the salary was $100k and the commission plan capped sales at $150k. But you got a Ford Taurus for a company car and they paid for your cell phone. "So what happens if I hit quota the first quarter and then close a million-dollar sale in the second quarter?" The answer was that I wouldn't make any commission on it. I seriously laughed at this response. There was no need to waste any more of our time.

Why would anybody hire a salesperson and then cap the compensation? That is very socialistic. That is illogical. Why would anybody even work after hitting quota? I realized why I always beat them. I left that interview even more fired up about competing against them. And to this day, I've never lost to them.

PROPOSED SOLUTION –
Do I even have to tell you this recommendation? Never EVER cap a salesperson. In fact, you should do the opposite. Once they hit their quota, give them escalators! If they were paid 10% commission, raise it to 15% or 20% for every dollar OVER quota. You DO want to grow your business – right?

PROBLEMS IDENTIFIED –
Too many quotas are unattainable AND unreasonable!

- Unless at least 20% of your salespeople are hitting the quota, chances are great that MANAGEMENT has the wrong quota, not that the sales force is inadequate.

- I've actually been in meetings when the management team was putting together a plan on how they will avoid paying the sales team by inflating the quotas.
- On Target Earnings (OTE) are the WORST compensation plans! 80% of the sales jobs I have left were after I was wildly successful only to be "punished" with a quota that more than DOUBLED. Increasing my quota and keeping my OTE the same meant my commission percentages decreased. Why would any company take a top performer and reduce their pay? I don't have any problem with increasing my quota as long as I have an opportunity to make MORE money, not LESS!

For those that are new to sales and haven't experienced this tactic, let me give you a real-life example:

You are hired with a salary of $150,000. You are told that the OTE will be $300,000 with a very realistic $1,000,000 quota your first year. This is what is called a 50/50 compensation plan where one half of your pay is salary and the other half is commission. Companies expect that a new salesperson will have a "ramp up time" so while $1,000,000 may seem low, they say this to hire top talent that are used to closing much more than that. So when over achievers close twice their quota numbers, escalator- incentives kicks in and we make great money…that first year.

Of course the quotas for your next year must be based upon your actual numbers PLUS the corporate growth objective. Right? Despite how much salespeople hate this fact, this is completely logical and is actually a very good business practice! But the kicker there is that the OTE never changes so no matter what the quota is, your salary will always be one half of your compensation. So $1,000,000 quota will earn you a $300,000 year. But when your quota is raised to $2,400,000, you will still make $300,000! So you will have to sell over twice as much in your second year to make the same amount of money as when you sold $1,000,000!

The readers that are good at math have already identified the problem. For those of you that aren't good at math, by raising the quota, they have reduced our commission percentages!

Example of two years with $2,000,000 in sales each year:
<u>50/50 Plan with an OTE of $300,000 and $1,000,000 quota</u>
Quota - $1,000,000
Salary - $150,000
Calculation - $150,000/$1,000,000 = **<u>15% commission rate</u>** for first million
Accelerators – Over $1,000,000 quota will be paid at 20% Actual Sales - $2,000,000
Calculation - $1,000,000 x 15% = $150,000 PLUS $1,000,000 x 20% = $200,000
Total Commission - $350,000 Plus $150,000 salary = **<u>$500,000 total pay</u>**

Sounds Great! Now watch what happens to an OTE plan when that $2,000,000 of actual sales plus 20% growth becomes the new quota:
50/50 Plan with an OTE of $300,000 and NEW $2,400,000 mil quota
Quota $2,000,000 + 20% growth = $2,400,000 quota
Salary - $150,000
Calculation - $150,000/$2,400,000 = **<u>6.25% commission rate</u>**
Accelerators – Over $2,400,000 quota will be paid at 10% Actual Sales - $2,000,000
Calculation - $2,000,000 x 6.25% = $125,000
Total Commission - $125,000 Plus $150,000 salary = **<u>$275,000 total pay</u>**

What I just described here is a $300,000 OTE comp plan that is a 50/50 plan with a salary of $150,000. The $300,000 number doesn't change regardless of the quota amount. When the quota was

$1,000,000, the commission rate was 15%. But when that quota is blown away so the actual revenue gets a growth rate added to it to make the new quota $2,400,000, the commission percentage drops significantly to 6.25%!

So success is punished on an OTE 50/50 plan, which has been the most popular plan I have been presented! If I sold $2,000,000 both years, the second year, my income would drop from
$500,000 to just $275,000.

What do you think good salespeople do when this happens? THEY LEAVE! I worked for a company that constantly **rehired** salespeople because they would get their new quotas, leave the company, got a new role with a new compensation plan, it happened there too so they went back to the previous role to start over again with a low compensation plan! I worked with a guy that was rehired FOUR times at the same company because he kept leaving just so he could "reset" his compensation plan each time he came back. Other people would just move around internally to get new comp plans. Thus proving once again that "Compensation Drives Behavior!"

I also worked for a company that loved OTE and knew people would leave. So they took a different approach to address this problem. It was a strict company policy that if you left the company, you could never come back. This struck fear into people that left because this company was also big into acquisitions and if you left and were acquired by this company, you would immediately be terminated regardless of your sales performance. OTEs are awful. The only way I will change my mind about this is if the OTE went up when the quotas increased. But I've never seen this happen.

PROPOSED SOLUTION –

Either OTE plans need to die, quotas need to stay the same (bad business move), or OTE ALSO needs to be adjusted when the quota is increased. Why won't this happen? Because those making the decision are also working their compensation plans! They are typically compensated on PROFIT so they are watching something called the COS (Cost of Sale) and these people view over achievers as "PAID TOO MUCH" versus "THEY BROUGHT IN THE SAME REVENUE AS TWO PEOPLE WOULD HAVE BROUGHT IN and actually SAVED money!" I mentioned earlier that financial people make the WORST sales leaders! This is a perfect example of why!

The glass is way fuller than it is empty by paying salespeople well. But few executives can see the soft dollar impact because the management layers between Execs and Sales are showing them hard dollar numbers. In addition, politics cloud the views.

My recommendation is that just as Fractional CFOs are big business, I believe Fractional Sales Leadership needs to be leveraged more often. Internal people have their own personal agendas and want the Emperor to think his clothes are there. An outsider like a Fractional Sales Leader will be able to tell the Emperor when he or she is naked without the politics and personal agendas clouding their message. This is another warning about the **ENC Syndrome**.

PROBLEM IDENTIFIED – Companies that believe sales organizations are a necessary evil will often assign unrealistic and/or unattainable quotas.

I was enticed to come aboard a software company and one of the promises made to me during the interview is that while the fiscal year was almost ½ over, because I would complete at least half a year, my quota would be prorated and I would actually qualify for their quota club. This was a huge reason why I accepted the job despite being told I would have to buy my own laptop. I exceeded my quota during those six months but I was denied the club trip because "too many people made it already." All these years later and I am still disappointed that I didn't get to go on that trip to Africa! It wasn't the only thing that I was denied at this company. This type of "anti-sales" culture is layered with issues. Several of my examples so far have been from this same company.

After working at this company for about four months, it was a running joke that if you have a huge commission coming, pack your office because they will try and find a reason to terminate you right before the deal closed.

Sound familiar?

NOTE: This was a slow quarter so the company offered a special "Double Bubble" commission payout to motivate a more aggressive attempt to close business. So my 11.33% commission was now paid at 22.66%. Because of this double commission payout, I had two deals about to close that were already in the clients' legal departments that would earn me $500k total commissions. As a joke, I had my office packed up.

I was actually terminated for the most bizarre reason you read about in the Preface. Here is the rest of the story I promised to share:

Despite being terminated, I never went a day unemployed because when I arrived home, my phone was ringing. It was my now former sales manager offering me a job with one of their top resellers/partners. He told me that he worried my two deals wouldn't close now that I was gone plus I was his top salesperson and he needed my help with the rest of the team. Therefore, he told the reseller that he was going to put all the deals currently being worked, through the partner as long as I was the one that co-sold with his team. In other words, he was explaining that I would now get credit for ALL sales, not just mine.

Sounds like a pretty good deal. Right? Not really. They wanted me to "help" the other salespeople (aka sell their deals for them) without compensating me as a manager AND because I was now with a reseller, they would still be able to avoid paying me that hefty "Double Bubble."

Because they were just the reseller, the partner could only pay me 8% of the profit! So instead of getting $500k (which was based upon the total sales price), I would get paid about $8k (based upon a profit of about 25% of the sales price)! This was a significant decrease in my commissions. Because the partner kept 92% of the profit after paying me 8%, they would make more than ME and I had spent MONTHS getting these two deals to the finish line!

It should come as no surprise that the company didn't respect my relationships with my clients. Again, this is a great example how people at the top, lose touch with reality at the field level. These were customers that had bought from me for 10 years and multiple companies so my relationships were solid. These are also the same clients I mentioned despised the company that I was representing because both had been burned by this company in the past.

When both clients heard what happened to me, they pulled both deals off the table. I accepted the role with the Partner so I wouldn't miss a paycheck but I immediately started interviewing for a job that wasn't connected to this awful company and I left just after a few months with the Partner.

These stories are an emotional beating. The lack of respect for salespeople that I have witnessed during my career is sad and it boggles my mind that it is even legal.

Salespeople are just pawns in a game of chess to companies. These tactics to avoid commission payouts will end up costing the company more in the long run. In fact, while I worked at this company, I actually spent more time trying to convince my clients that the company was not as bad as its reputation. They not only treated salespeople poorly, they treated clients with the same disrespect. In fact, some of the Execs ended up going to jail just a few years after I left.

PROPOSED SOLUTION -

Most of my "Memoirs" are about things that are broken but this time I want to share a story about one of the best Executive Leadership moves I have seen in my career. I like to leave out company names but, in this case, I wish I could tell you the name of the company because what the CEO did was remarkable and I've never seen it done again. This story is about a start-up company and the CEO was a man I truly admired.

It was a Sales Kick-off meeting. Only one person legitimately hit the quota number (me). You could feel the low morale in the room. The kickoff meeting started with a motivational video and the Key Note Speaker was a man that beat incredible odds to climb a mountain. It was inspirational yet you could still see and feel the defeat that was felt by the salespeople in the room when he was finished with his wonderful speech.

After the man left the stage, the next speaker was the CEO. As he solemnly approached the Podium, his first slide showed all the actual revenue numbers versus the sales quotas and revenue objectives. It was painfully obvious that we missed our targeted sales objectives by quite a bit which added to the tension in the room.

He then did the unspeakable; he took accountability!! No, he didn't say the low sales were his fault. Instead, he explained that since it was the company's first year, there were no baseline numbers from which to build logical quotas. He then said that he and his leadership team blew it when they assigned the original quotas. He then showed the rankings of sales force and focused in on the top 20%. He said that in his experience, the top 20% are always going to produce realistic numbers and he believed in the sales team he had put together.

His next slide showed the original quota numbers and NEW REVISED quota numbers! HE LOWERED THE QUOTA! He then announced that the top 20% were being recognized as the first recipients of the Quota Achievement Club! You could feel the rush of shock, disbelief, and excitement flood the room. The audience burst into applause. Even those that didn't make the top 20% were rejuvenated by his style of leadership! The bottom 80% were truly happy for those that were recognized and we all celebrated as a company. This sales kick-off transformed from a depression into a very high energy, well received, and dynamic event. Leadership truly earned respect and loyalty with this approach.

As I mentioned in Chapter One, so much of sales is psychological. Sales are beaten down and rejected daily. When they know their company is behind them, they take the beatings in stride. However, when the company is causing some of the beatings, it becomes a toxic culture that will spread in their industry and will cause image issues and lost sales. **Treat sales right and they will treat clients right and the marketplace will notice!**

Again, this attitude must start at the top. PAY US, RECOGNIZE US and BE HAPPY ABOUT IT!

PROBLEM IDENTIFIED –
We are SALESPEOPLE, not Rocket Scientists. Please keep our comp plans simple!

If people from one of my previous employers are reading this, they are probably laughing right now. One of the first things I was tasked to do at one of my most recent sales leadership roles was to find out what was broken and fix the comp plan. I was later told that they referred to the compensation plan that I proposed as a "Shit Show." The Owner's words, not mine. So apparently, I was part of the problem of creating overly complicated compensation plans. I can't argue with that. I mentioned in the Preface that I'm far from perfect. But I do try and learn from my mistakes and this will never happen again. But one thing that I definitely did RIGHT was to go speak with every single department at the company and I asked every person what they perceived to be broken. And let me tell you how enlightening it is when accounting tells you what is broken in sales versus what technical resources say is broken. This feedback was VERY different than what the inside and field sales reps told me!

PROPOSED SOLUTION -

As you make decisions around compensation plans, whom are YOU asking for input? Try asking each department for their observations. This is an excellent exercise and is extremely eye opening!

The best compensation plan I remember was a set percentage. Hunters were paid at 11.33% commission with certain quarters that paid out at 22.66% commissions. Don't ask me how they got those numbers. The important thing is that this was in the 90's and I still remember those numbers. They were generous commission rates and I loved them. Regardless of the quota, the commission percentages remained the same. There were no debates, everybody knew what their checks would look like, no secret formulas, no surprises, and no complicated math needed.

The reality is that most companies are not that simple. But at least go into it with this simplistic mindset so sales will be able to spend more time selling than trying to figure out how much they will make on each opportunity. Again – bring in a fractional sales leadership company to help you devise a simple and appropriate comp plan for your business! Don't rely on salespeople or your own employees to create it because their personal agendas may get in the way of producing the best one for your company but DO get their feedback.

Creating the right compensation plan is the most important thing a company can do and yet, not enough time is spent on creating them!

PROBLEM IDENTIFIED –
Too many companies try and figure out ways to not pay commissions.

I worked for a private company that was almost a billion-dollar empire owned and run by a dictator. He didn't even try to hide the fact that he resented paying sales commissions because that money literally came out of his pocket. I had a VP title but I was only a puppet and I was not allowed to think for myself. As you can imagine, this was the most miserable job of my life but it was also the highest six-figure salary I've ever received so it was difficult to quit.

I had some of the most incredible salespeople on my team. I cared about them and I fought for them on a daily basis. As soon as a salesperson developed a healthy pipeline, the CEO would suddenly have HR call me to fire them. Sometimes he even called me himself to tell me to fire people on my team! The excuse was always the same; the salesperson ran out of time.

And this company didn't just mess with sales PEOPLE, they also went to great extremes to not pay LEADERSHIP as well. This same company had ME on a compensation plan that had this criteria – I had to work an entire quarter to receive my bonus. My start date was supposed to be July 1. However, I received a call that something was wrong with my paperwork and I couldn't start until July 2nd. I didn't think anything about it at the time. I ended up hitting my numbers that first quarter but as I researched to find out why I hadn't received my bonus, I was told that I didn't work the entire quarter since I started on July 2nd vs 1st. I suddenly understood the REAL reason my paperwork was delayed. This was a $30,000 bonus lost because they started me a day late!

I could just imagine the CEO laughing with glee over this because he believed he was intellectually superior to those that worked for him. And he is right because it never crossed my mind that someone would be this ruthless and greedy.

And this isn't even the big thing they did to me. There were days that I felt like I literally was working for SATAN. The last quarter of the year was a blow out for my team so my bonus was going to be really good. I received a call the day before Christmas Eve telling me that there was going to be a reorg and my role was being eliminated so effective immediately I would no longer be employed there. However, I would receive severance for the next few months.

Most people would be devastated to learn that they lost their job on Christmas Eve EVE. But I was so happy! I actually had to work Thanksgiving Day at this company and my request for time off during Christmas had been denied as well. And since this was the most corrupt place I had ever worked, I was thrilled that they were going to pay me through the New Year so I could rest and actually enjoy my family during the holiday without having work stress to contend with!

WRONG.

Because they laid me off on December 23rd, I didn't get to complete my quarter so I got my nice six figure salary for the next few months but I didn't get my whopper of a bonus, which was WAY more than

that severance package!
Can you believe some of these stories? I couldn't make this stuff up if I tried. And the sad thing is that I know my readers have their own stories that are similar to mine. **THIS HAS TO CHANGE!**

PROPOSED SOLUTION –
My advice here is to salespeople, not leadership. When you have a privately held company run by a person like this, no advice will matter. In fact, they will never even bother reading a book like this because their greed far surpasses their desire to learn. You can't win. So my advice is to do your homework before you waste your time. You do not want to fill funnels for someone that will never appreciate your contributions. They will spend way too much time trying to find ways to never pay you.

The crazy thing about this Dictator is that many deals never closed because the terminated salespeople developed genuine relationships with the clients. **Clients know that when a company treats employees like this, clients are not treated any better.** I see deals lost all the time because of sales turnover.

Inspirational Quote -

"Success isn't just about what you accomplish in your life, it's about what you INSPIRE others to do."

CHAPTER 5 -
"Noise" Will Kill Motivation and Focus!

He got a new sales manager...I don't think it's going well...

PROBLEM IDENTIFIED –
Noise is an unspoken career and revenue killer.

As I was in the middle of writing this chapter, a former employee called to tell me about his new company. He just completed three days of training and at the conclusion of the training, the CEO came in to address the 14 new sales hires. He told them that 50% of them would quit within the first 30 or 60 days. So in order to save everybody time and money, he offered them each $2500 if they will quit by this Friday.

Are you kidding me?!

What a great way to create "noise" in the heads of brand-new people that should be focused on tactical execution strategies. Instead, they now know that 50% of them are predicted to fail...BY THE CEO!

So as I type this, my former sale rep is talking to me on my cell phone and he is freaking out. He is actually talking himself into taking the $2500! What was this CEO thinking? He just took 14 people that he flew in from all over the country. These people should be fired up to hit the streets and start selling and instead, he has damaged their confidence and has them all wondering if they should quit instead of wasting their time building their pipelines. I wonder if this CEO has ever heard of "self-fulfilled-prophecies?" This screams "SALES IS A NECESSARY EVIL!" Normally I try and encourage people but this says nothing good about the company culture so I have no choice but to advice this poor guy to take the money and keep interviewing. Geez.

Mentor Tip for Fellow Sales Pros –
"'Noise' in your head is a success killer. "
~ Kimberlee Slavik, Author of Memoirs of An Angry Sales Pro – Sales Leadership MUST change!

UPDATE – Six weeks later, this same employee text me that 13 out of the 14 new hires were just terminated. So I'm no genius that that is way more than the 50% attrition the CEO predicted on that last day of training. I wish I could share the company name so all the readers know to steer clear of that company! My friend feels badly for several of his co-workers because they had left pretty good jobs to take this one. I can relate!

"Noise" in your head is a success killer and this story proves the point. However, I think the noise this time was actually in the CEO's head! While management and culture typically trigger the noise, only you can control your thoughts. Sadly once the noise starts, it's extremely difficult to turn it off. One trick that has worked well for me is to go interview at other companies. You will either realize that the grass is not as green on the other side of the fence as you thought, OR you will find a better job. Either way, this will help stop the noise so you can regain the focus you need to be successful.

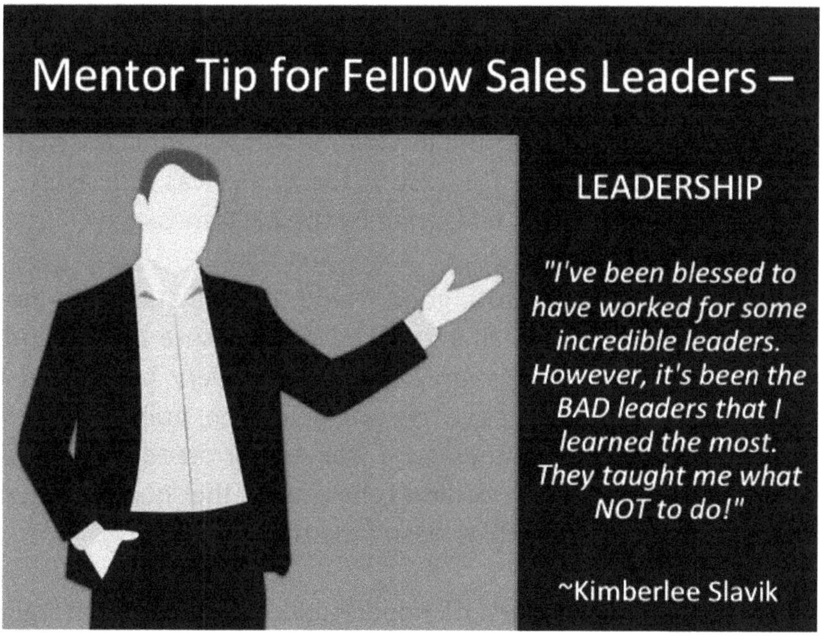

Mentor Tip for Fellow Sales Leaders –
LEADERSHIP
"I've been blessed to have worked for some incredible leaders. However, it's been the BAD leaders that I learned the most. They taught me what NOT to do!"
~Kimberlee Slavik

Here is one of the funniest "bad leadership" stories that ever happened to me; I was working for a company based in Georgia and I worked from Texas so most of our meetings were conducted as video web conference calls. In this role, I was not only accountable for sales; I was also an operations manager and was expected to ensure my territory was profitable. In fact, my compensation plan was tied to the profitability of the territory. Needless to say, I was definitely incented to keep my expenses under control.

One day, I was leading a videoconference with a potential new client. I had several people from corporate on the conference call as well. My actual VP of Sales was in yet another state and he was sharing his desktop (TIP - Never share your entire desktop – always share a specific application during a call like this!) with everybody on the call and conducting a demo for the client. Suddenly, the CEO sent an instant message to the VP of Sales and it popped up on the screen for me and everybody else to see, "Do you think Kim will be upset when she finds out we hired another person without telling her? She's not going to make as much money as we told her during the interview because it will impact her profits and commission plan." I then saw the VP of Sale's curser go to the instant messenger application on his desktop and shut it down. The rest of the demo was a disaster. The VP of Sales was obviously a bit rattled by the CEOs message.

My customer, who was also a good friend, immediately text me on my cell phone during the call and asked if I was sure he should buy from this company because they didn't seem very bright and the software wasn't very impressive. He was being very polite and he was laughing at what we all witnessed. I was embarrassed he saw what the CEO messaged but I couldn't help see the humor in what happened. I was also grateful it wasn't me that did it!

Because of my own history of imperfection, I am pretty forgiving when people make mistakes like this. The real problem in this scenario is that I was being held accountable for running a P&L (profit and loss), which I love doing and it was a huge reason I wanted this position. **However, you can't hold people accountable and not**

empower them to make decisions in a role like that. The biggest concern I had over that instant message was why did they exclude me from the hiring and decision-making process? Did they not trust me? This move didn't exactly help build my trust in THEM.

Inspirational Quote -

"When the wrong people leave your life, the right things start happening."

After the meeting was over, my client called me to tell me that he was concerned for me and my career. He let me know that while he loved working with me, he was never going to buy from this company. He elaborated for about fifteen minutes about why he felt this company and the product were beneath me and he highly recommended that I not waste my time here. The observation he made that stung the most was that the leadership on the call that was supposed to be there to HELP me, actually just cost me the sale. Did I really want to embarrass myself again by contacting my other loyal clients and risk the same outcome?

That single instant message from the CEO triggered noise in the heads of my VP of Sales (he stumbled through the demo), my client, and myself. This is just one example how "noise" can be easily triggered by poor leadership. And sadly, once the noise starts, it is incredibly difficult to shut it down.

After that meeting, nobody even called me or tried to explain the instant message that popped up during the client conference call. I honestly think they were hoping that I didn't see the CEO's instant message. Maybe they thought I was too dumb to care.

I wasn't sure I could respect or trust any of these leaders. So I gave my resignation the next day. And I admit that I enjoyed telling them that I did, indeed, see the instant message and so did my client. I also offered to train them on how to share an application versus their entire desktops during a videoconference so that didn't happen again in the future. They never took me up on my offer.

This is also the same company that didn't have software license agreements and was actually a reseller of another company's intellectual property. So my decision to resign was not solely based upon the mishap with the CEO's instant message. This company and the leadership were quickly demonstrating a pattern of deception and I didn't want to be "guilty by association." Plus, as the CEO pointed out, I wasn't going to make the type of money I was promised during the interview. I made a bad decision to accept this job offer.

This story was not some sort of therapeutic rant; this was an effort to share specific types of thoughts that will distract salespeople from selling. I shared all those details so you could read the extensive amount of thoughts that can be swirling around in your salespeople's heads when they are subjected to poor leadership.

Noise is seldom, if ever, discussed but it's been my experience that this is a huge problem and it is extremely costly for all concerned. Bad leadership causes a LOT of noise which is why it is so critical to have an excellent leadership team in place that can coach, guide, mentor, nurture, inspire, and help the sales teams be successful.

Bad leadership will distract from constructive and productive activities and cause what I call, **INVISIBLE CHAOS, which is really**

what 'noise' is. Pay attention to it and I challenge every leader reading this book to attempt to tie a cost to it. I suspect you will discover it is far more expensive than you ever imagined.

Watching leadership make dumb decisions can also trigger noise. Salespeople constantly observe, analyze, and discuss the various mistakes they witness by leadership. I can't tell you how many times it felt like we were living a real-life version of "***The Emperor's New Clothes***" I referred to this earlier as ***The ENC Syndrome***. How can the King (leadership) be so obviously naked and he doesn't think we can see it?

PROBLEM IDENTIFIED – Politicians make Execs look stupid.

One major way to disrupt the focus of a sales organization is to hire a politician to lead them. This is one of the most common mistakes I have seen during my career. Over half of all the sales leaders that I have reported to had very limited sales experience and even less sales **leadership** experience. But they were terrific at politics.

There is no better way to cripple and demotivate a sales organization than to put a politician in a sales leadership role because the noise it creates is deafening.

These politician personalities constantly smile, are a ray of sunshine and will tell anybody anything they want to hear. Salespeople can smell these Con Artists a mile away and feel instant distrust for them as leaders.

And "noise" starts flooding the thoughts of salespeople, which reduces the focus on sales planning and execution.

One of the main traits of a politician is the inability to be forthcoming with messages from above to the sales organization. They have a difficult time delivering bad news or standing up for their team. They care more about their own career than those around them, which gives them the tendency to take credit for others' accomplishments.

Politicians also tend to be self-absorbed. They love to hear themselves speak and are terrible listeners. They tend to "know it all." When they are given advice, it will eventually become their own ideas.

These people are experts at "managing UP." They have ZERO desire to manage DOWN because the driving force behind everything they do is based upon "what's in it for ME?" Which is why their team can't stand to work for them.

When a politician is hired to lead a sales organization, respect for the entire chain above them is destroyed because it becomes very visible that the company's top leaders were duped.

Two of the most blatant politicians I know today are constantly posting photos on social media "promoting" their current companies. But they are both in every single photo. The **"ENC Syndrome"** strikes again. Why can't Execs see that this is making a laughing stock out of them and the politician? Why can't they see that this is SELF promotion versus promotion for the company? Why can't they see that these Con Artists are making themselves the "face" of the company which will make it almost impossible to ever get rid of them without fall out and confusion in the marketplace?

I was asked to have lunch with one of these politicians and give feedback. He was extremely likeable. He told me how well connected he was. He promised he could help my sales team get in doors that we currently couldn't get open. So he was appealing to me as well. It was impossible to truly articulate or justify my gut feelings for this man; I didn't like or trust him. But it seemed more like the decision was already made so why did they really want my feedback? Was HE really assessing ME? What if I gave my real impression of him and was wrong and he really could generate a huge amount of revenue with his connections? Furthermore, if he was able to do all the things he claimed, why did they need ME? All of these questions flying around in my head are "noise."

The result was that this man was hired. He was suddenly shadowing me on everything. He was disruptive during my team meetings. He offered zero value, he didn't make one single introduction as he promised. The entire sales team observed that he would disappear at events and he always had a boastful story about whom he was with and what he was going to get them to do. Yet nobody on my team had one good meeting because of him despite all of his promises during the interview process.

Everywhere I turned, he was there and he was listening to every single thing I was saying to the sales team. Why? Was he assessing my abilities? Was he learning? It was just a few days later, I heard he was bringing incredible ideas to the Executive Team...MY ideas but presenting them as HIS. Yep. We had a politician in our midst.

To validate my suspicions, I made a call to an employee at his previous company to invite him to apply for an open role I had on my team. I asked if he was aware that his former leader now worked with us. I suggested that perhaps he might be interested in following him here. The young man I spoke with was wise beyond his years and was very diplomatic but he made it very clear that the company was thrilled this politician was gone. This young man told me that the culture was doing much better. He continued explaining that people that were ignored during his leadership were suddenly getting recognized and promoted. Opportunities were now at an all-time high and without saying the actual words, it was clear to me that our new politician didn't have the respect of the people that formerly worked for him and nobody wanted to leave to follow him. Beware the **ENC Syndrome**.

This Organization Chart clearly shows that I reward employees that worship me.

Nobody wants to work for politicians but Executives tend to fall for their tactics because they know how to feed the Executive Level Egos. I also think this is due to the disconnect Execs have with their people that are working on the front lines.

Politicians are incredibly destructive but they are so likeable that you can't make yourself get rid of them. They seem to always have a story of extreme optimism and future success to share but rarely do they ever show results. But when they are gone, you can FEEL the environment change from fake to real. When a politician leaves, people often start comparing stories and uncover false stories, inaccurate forecasts, ideas that were misrepresented, just to name a few. I have observed these types of people also tend to abuse alcohol and are able to hide it well. There really isn't much substance to these types of people.

But here is the damage done to the sales organization – most salespeople will leave under this type of leadership. They have nobody to go to about their concerns because the people above this person HIRED him or her. And these Execs tend to sing their praises non-stop and totally buy into all their claims and promises. In addition, most employees have experienced these scenarios in the past and they know that telling senior level leaders that they made a bad hire tends to backfire on the messenger. Therefore, people quietly start looking for new jobs. By the time the company figures out what is happening, the damage is done and an entire sales organization and sales leadership will have to be rebuilt from scratch. The true cost of this hiring mistake is difficult to assess because a lot of costs are associated with time. New hire ramp up time, ignored pipelines, company credibility, and client confusion over a new staff, are just some examples of the cost of turning over a sales organization.

PROPOSED SOLUTION – POLITICIANS MAKE THE WORST SALES LEADERS! DO NOT HIRE THEM - EVER!

Today most people know that it is illegal to say anything bad about a former employee but their reaction to being asked to come aboard will speak volumes. If someone is less than interested in having someone as a leader for a second time, take that as a sign that something was wrong.

A VERY simple thing to do is go look for recommendations on their LinkedIn profile. How many former employees have taken time to document why they liked working for this person? Why isn't this a standard step in the hiring process for sales leadership?

Never rely on the references that candidates give you when making any hiring decisions. Nobody will ever give you bad references. Instead, make an effort to conduct your own research. Calling former direct reports is a good way to get a pulse on what type of leader you are considering. If people are eager to follow him or her, chances are good that you made a good hire but if there are excuses and reluctance or if they describe a company that is now doing well, you may be about to hire a reject or a problem.

Furthermore, if one of these people claim to have great relationships, challenge them to setup some introduction meetings to see just how well people accept them BEFORE you hire them.

I think it's interesting that on the same day I was writing this chapter, I received a call from one of my friends that works for the city. She told me that a very high-ranking official was fired that same day. When I asked her why, her response was that he was just a politician. She continued explaining that there was little substance behind him and he was extremely self-absorbed. I thought this was so relevant because it doesn't matter if a politician is hired as a Sales Leader or a Government Official, people are relieved when they leave. THIS is when people will start sharing why they didn't trust them.

Politics is not just a personality trait; sometimes politics in the workplace is a more literal issue. And in today's world of intolerance of different political beliefs, this just can't be allowed.

I did some consulting for a private company in Naples, Florida and the CEO actually sent out emails to his entire company demanding that they vote for a specific party. My mind still can't wrap around how any leader could justify taking this approach with his employees. It would never fly with a publicly traded company but this CEO owned this company and didn't hesitate to fire people that didn't share his political viewpoints. This was a dictatorship culture with few happy and productive employees. There is a website called "Glassdoor" that is full of anonymous commentary from existing and former employees that constantly complain about companies like this one. So if you think it doesn't matter, you are wrong. Top talent will look at sites like this and never bother pursuing a career there. Only desperate people will be applying. How much does THAT cost a company?

But the politics that are more disastrous are the internal ones. One of the Fortune 50 companies I worked for, had one of the strongest "Good Ole' Boy" networks I have ever seen. None of these men were superstars but they had each other's backs unconditionally. I saw some of the dumbest operational processes of my life come from this group. Here is an example of one of their policies that negatively impacted sales in a huge way:

I was a regular keynote speaker at various events that included both the direct sales teams and also the indirect sales teams of our various partners. I always made a point to ask what we could do better and I was consistently told that they rarely received any sales leads and the few they did get, were so old that the competition had already closed the deals and the leads were dead. This was so ridiculous that I didn't believe it initially. So I researched and I sincerely wish I could share the flow chart describing the lead validation process that one of the "Good Ole' Boys" had created and actually won numerous awards for developing.

But it looked an awful like the one in this cartoon! In fact it's so similar that this cartoon had to have been drawn by someone that actually saw it!

None of our leads ever close which is hard to understand when you look at this twelve month qualification process we go through before we give them to sales.

The flow chart these Good Ole' Boys guarded showed a lead going through over 20 different verifications before getting sent to sales of any kind. Leads could take from four months to a year to get in the hands of the sales force!

When I asked why this was implemented, I was told that they had a huge problem that this solved; the salespeople were constantly complaining that leads they received were bad so this process eliminated those complaints. I couldn't help laugh at how out of touch with reality this leadership team was with what good salespeople DO!

Did they really not know that the reason the complaints stopped was because the sales leads stopped?!

What a Pipe Dream Looks Like...

Wouldn't you rather be an Order Taker than waste all of your time selling?

They continued to explain the need for this flowchart was to ensure that each lead was verified to protect the valuable time of the salespeople. But when I asked who was doing the qualifying, I was told that wasn't important.

Seriously?

Based upon this type of logic, I could tell that none of these men ever carried a sales quota or were effective sales professionals. So why in the world were they allowed to make major decisions that impacted the entire sales organization?

When I developed and presented an alternative process (which was a standard every place I have worked) the response I received was to back down because I didn't understand the politics involved with this current system. When I asked them to educate me on this, I was told that it was "above my pay grade" and to forget about it.

I never did uncover the "politics" but it really isn't important in this story. When politics inhibit the sales organization, or becomes the number one complaint from sales, it has to be addressed.

Thankfully a new CEO flushed out this Good Ole' Boy system and they were all terminated. It was incredible how fast leads suddenly were in sales hands when the REAL "political" issue was eliminated.

A year after I left his company, a competitor told me that they actually had a copy of that flow chart and the competition LOVED it (for obvious reasons) and this lead flow chart made a laughing stock out of the leadership team in the marketplace.

Please put away that purchase order Mr. Customer. You can't possibly be ready to buy yet because I haven't gone through our entire sales process yet!

Side note on this topic – This must be a rampant issue because as I searched for cartoons on this subject, they were in abundance. In fact, there were more artists making fun of lead generation processes than any other topic in this book! I hope each sales leader puts down this book right now and goes and investigates their current lead tracking process!

PROPOSED SOLUTION –

I keep saying that a sales profession is an extremely emotional career path. Salespeople need to be asked what is broken. They want to be heard. They want to know they matter. They need to know leadership at all levels sincerely cares and then they need to see action taken on their suggestions. When was the last time you listened to your salespeople's concerns? When was the last time you actually asked them for input????

The best cultures will ensure that sales know that they are the reason every other job exists and that every single employee in the company is cheering for them when they succeed.

One of the readers of the draft really took issue with this comment every single time I stated it. His question was, "In earlier chapters you talked about companies where the product did not in fact exist, so is there any relationship between creating a good product being a reason every other job exists?"

I'm glad he asked this. His question actually clarifies when I would point out that the actual thing being sold was a "vision to the investors." And yes. Selling this vision and getting money from investors is exactly why all the other jobs existed! Great question!

In my story above, the sales organization, including resellers and partners, kept telling leadership that the marketing lead process was broken. Yet nobody took action. Why not? Salespeople are some of the company's best sources of information because they are dealing with the clients on a daily basis and feel competitive pressures and know details that upper management will rarely experience first-hand. Wise leaders will leverage that knowledge and experience to make their company better!

Poor Guy. Corporate said they have a sales friendly culture. So he shared his thoughts and they fired him.

Remember this cartoon from Chapter One? Few companies I have worked for had a BELIEVABLE Open-Door Policy that encouraged blunt and honest discussions. We tend to believe that if we say anything that is perceived as negative, we will be terminated so we keep our heads down and keep plugging away. This has to change because salespeople are some of the most insightful and creative people in any organization.

The last thing salespeople need is for any political behaviors to impede their success. I wish I could find a company that had a zero policy for political behaviors but we are human and politics are impossible to eliminate totally. However, improving communication will help. Ensuring that the sales organization knows they can give honest feedback without fear of retribution is critical when establishing a sales-friendly culture.

I should be able to tell you that your baby is ugly and you look me in the eye and acknowledge the truth in that statement and then ASK how we work together to address it! And I better be prepared to offer some suggestions!

I know people that are excellent at pointing out all the things that are broken. These people are a dime a dozen. So having guidelines in place such as requiring that any problems identified should also have several suggestions for improvements is an excellent criteria to instill in every employee. Expectations should be made crystal clear that employees should not come to the table with problems unless they have some suggestions how to improve or eliminate those problems.

Why is there a bag covering our baby's head? Clearly she is the most beautiful baby in the nursery! She looks exactly like US!

PROBLEM IDENTIFIED – Don't over communicate!

I have to admit that this is an area in which I struggle. I take great pride in the fact that my goal is to provide a transparent leadership style. I want to tell my team what is going on so they know I respect them and that I trust them.

Furthermore, I think it helps individuals grow professionally. More importantly, I want them to know they can trust me to not be secretive. However, I have seen first-hand that over communication can cause "noise" in their heads and will keep them from staying focused on doing their jobs.

PROPOSED SOLUTION –
The more positive information that filters to the sales organization, the more likely they will keep a positive attitude and stay focused.

Tell them what they need to know to be better at their jobs but shield them from unnecessary negativity that could distract them or make them lose their focus. This all sounds so easy and logical but when you are a mid-level manager, who else can you talk to about certain topics than your own sales team? It's almost impossible to resist this temptation.

Remember that social media is a powerful outlet. Angry or bitter employees will hurt your company's chances at recruiting quality people.

I've mentioned mentoring multiple times in this book because it solves a lot of problems. Mentoring people outside of my company has become an outlet for me to get things off of my chest without impacting my own team. Of course nothing that could hurt the company or break my confidentiality agreement is ever discussed. I also try to have my own mentors that I can ask advice. These outside relationships are a good way to discuss various scenarios and get an outsiders unbiased perspective. Mentoring is not a one-way street. Both participants have the opportunity to bounce things off of each other. I highly recommend this regardless of the role you have during your career.

The Power of Mentorship Programs –
One of the challenges within an organization is that people are often scared to talk openly with anybody in the company. Again, politics are a scary thing and you just never know who you can trust. More frequently than not, trusting someone that you work with can be risky because it can blow up in your face. This is a great example of

why I am a huge believer in mentoring programs!

men·tor·ship ˈmentôrSHip,ˈmentərSHip/ noun

1. the guidance provided by a mentor, especially an experienced person in a company or educational institution. "he is revered by his employees for his mentorship and problem-solving qualities"
- a period of time during which a person receives guidance from a mentor. "a two-year mentorship with an entrepreneur in a tech start-up"

The definition of mentoring sounds so simple but it is so much more than that! In the past week, I have been blessed to speak with and mentor eight different people. All are going through different things. Some of them I have known for years, others were complete strangers that found me through the LinkedIn Mentorship program. (Which I highly endorse!)

What makes these mentor relationships so powerful is that we don't work together. This gives them a "safe" ear. I am someone that can't hurt them or gossip about our discussion. What we discuss is 100% confidential. They are free to say things to me that they can't possibly articulate to coworkers.

And what is great for ME, is that this gives ME a "safe" ear as well. But it is also a great opportunity to be a true leader. When I am leading at work, I have to be "Politically Correct" at all times. I have to worry that what I say could get someone in trouble, including myself.

I have to worry that I will offend or say something to make them want to resign. But what is most impactful for me is that their decision to execute or not execute my advice will not have a direct impact on MY performance.

Mentor Tip for Fellow Sales Pros –
"Get A Mentor. BE A Mentor."
~ Kimberlee Slavik, Author of Memoirs of An Angry Sales Pro – Sales Leadership MUST change!

Being a sales leader is extremely difficult. You know what your team needs to do to be successful. You can advise and coach but if they don't execute your guidance and they fail, YOU fail. And since your own job is dependent upon your team's execution, coaching at work can be emotional. And once emotions are engaged, it can cloud or distort your own decision-making. With mentorship, there is no impact on your own performance so it is extremely easy to be objective, cerebral, and completely honest with your advice.

Furthermore, coaching others in this "safe" mentoring environment helps you clear your own head professionally. For example, I had a young man come to me and tell me that he accepted a job offer because he had his own professional goal and plan to get to the next level quickly. However, management decisions impacted his plans and set him back several years. He asked me what to do. I asked him if he had a coach and champion within his organization. He told me that when he accepted the job, he had a strong one. But the organizational change eliminated his coach and champion and he really didn't have anybody there that had a vested interest in his goals or his success.

This was a no-brainer for me. I reminded him that he is his own corporation and just as any corporation, if there are obstacles in the way, you must either eliminate the obstacles or figure what is best for the corporation. I encouraged him to never allow someone else to control his destiny. Because of this advice, the young man resigned and took a higher position with a different company. As I reflected on our conversation, I realized that I also was in a similar situation and I had been battling internally if I should be humble and patient, or if I should leave. I realized that had I been mentoring myself, I would have advised myself to leave. So I did.

Another example of this type of mentorship is in another blog I have posted on LinkedIn called, "Career Advice to My Millennial Son." After listening to an ethical dilemma my son was describing to me, I realized I was in a very similar situation but I was blind to it. Listening to my son's struggle gave me the ability to see my own situation with better clarity. Once again, I resigned.

If you aren't mentoring someone today, I highly recommend that you find time to mentor as many people as you can. I currently mentor eighteen people of all ages and I must add that these conversations are some of the highlights of my week and I look forward to each and every one of them. When I see someone succeed after taking my advice, we both celebrate. Passing along years of wisdom to someone else is a natural behavior. And it is humbling when you realize that even with all your own experience, it is so easy to be blind to the mistakes you are making in your own career. And every person I mentor teaches ME something new every time we speak. They don't always ask for advice, sometimes they just want to brag about something new they tried that worked. I have been inspired to try some of the things at my own job and was delighted when I also saw positive results!

I would love to read YOUR stories on mentoring. Did someone help YOU? Do you have your own success story to share? Please email memoirs@dynaexec.com.

Thank you and happy mentoring!

CHAPTER 6 –
Commissions are a Part of Payroll, They Aren't a Slush Fund!

PROBLEM IDENTIFIED –
The majority of salespeople I know have had commissions taken from them so the company can report better earnings! "Compensation Drives Behavior" and most Execs are bonused based upon profits. Explains a lot, doesn't it?

So now I am going to contradict what I just said in Chapter 4. While we don't want or need distractions or "noise" in our heads, we also need honesty.

I had hit my annual quota and was working on a huge deal that was going to pay me escalators. When this opportunity closed, I would make over $750,000 in commissions. I was on a conference call with our CFO and her assistant as we ran over my financial numbers to ensure we maximized the profits and still could help the client justify the costs with a solid and quantifiable Return-On-Investment (ROI).

After several hours crunching numbers, we were calling it a night and I said my good-byes. As I was hanging up the phone, I heard the CFO say, "Wait! One more thing!" I stopped the hanging up process and put the phone back up to my ear and she began asking her assistant if they could make payroll next month. I was horrified because I knew instantly that I was not supposed to hear this! But if I hung up now, they would hear the click and they would know that I heard the CFOs question…so I waited.

There was a short pause before the assistance answered, "If Kimberlee closes this before the end of the month, we can factor (sell the contract to a financial institution for cash) the paper and we will be fine." The CFO then asked, "And if not…?" The response was, "We will have to lay off about 50 employees." I was distraught at this possibility but I was also realizing that I may not get my $750,000 commission!

First of all, every compensation plan I've ever received had something in them that allowed the company to adjust compensation plans at any time. So my first thought was, "Why would they pay me $750,000 when our finances are clearly not in good shape?" I knew my $14 million-dollar contract would save 50 jobs but it sounded like the company really needed that $750,000 as well. As this conversation was happening, I recall thinking that I should offer to let them pay out my commissions; especially if it would save jobs of people that I actually cared about!

It was shortly after this last comment that the final good-byes were made and I waited to hear both lines click off before I finally hung up.

So now that I was aware of the financial distress of the company, I became concerned and legitimately so. Remember the phone message fiasco I described in the Preface? Well, this is the rest of that story; It was just a few days after this phone call that the Senior VP of Sales started hammering me to get this deal in ASAP. And it was just a few days later that I got the call from my new VP of Sales about my territory changing. So was it really because of that phone recording that my deal was taken from me and I was banned from speaking with the client? Or was this a convenient excuse to keep from paying me that commission? Nobody ever knew what I overheard the CFO say to her assistant that day.

Had they just been honest with me about the financial crisis the company was experiencing, I would have been eager to help! Instead, they seemed to suddenly treat me as though I was the enemy as an attempt to keep from paying me that huge commission. The result was that their top salesperson left. And my phone rang constantly as all the other salespeople wondered why a salesperson would leave in the middle of a multi-million-dollar transaction unless something was seriously wrong? I couldn't tell anybody the truth or details about what happened. Although I had been banned from speaking with the client, I actually didn't WANT to communicate with the client because I didn't want to be accused of sabotaging the deal after I left.

Imagine what would have been going through my mind if I hadn't heard that conversation between the CFO and her assistant? I might have viewed things much more personally than I did. Others had sued this company. Because I knew this additional financial information, I left quietly.

There have been times at other companies when management

appeared to be somewhat incompetent or insane because of decisions we saw being made. However, once I considered that financial pressures may be causing these decisions to be made, my perspective completely changed.

Contrary to popular belief, not all salespeople are money hungry, selfish jerks. If we are treated like business professionals, most of us will behave and think like business professionals. Until we prove otherwise, why can't management assume the best about us?

While over communicating can be a problem, under communicating can also create distracting noise caused by jumping to the wrong conclusions. So treat your sales team as professionals and as adults and it will go a long way.

One of the most unusual things I have witnessed in my career was something Mark Hurd did February 2009. Normally, I don't mention company names but this is so public, it is pointless to try and pretend I'm not talking about HP.

The economy had crashed. HP stocks dropped 10%. 100,000 nervous employees assumed layoffs were inevitable. However, Mark held an all-hands meeting and predicted the economic downturn would be temporary and he explained that lay-offs would hurt the company because he believed they would have to turn around and rehire all those terminated positions in just a few months. However, he continued explaining that all employees would need to sacrifice to keep everybody's jobs. His solution was to immediately decrease the benefits and all salaries would be reduced by 5% - 20%. I was on this call and I remember the relief I felt knowing that I was only going to lose 10% of my pay versus 100% of my pay.

Because of these employee sacrifices, Hurd's bonus was $30 million that year based upon an extremely profitable year. Because Mark did an incredible job articulating the business reasons behind his decisions, HP had a great year despite a horrific economic downturn, the employees kept their jobs, and the company survived when many others did not do as well.

Mark gave every employee a huge gift by being so open and honest and for educating every single person about the company business by giving us all a peek into the tough decisions CEOs have to make on a daily basis. Are you giving your teams this same gift by having this level of communication? It sends a strong message that you respect them and trust them.

Mentor Tip for Fellow Sales Pros –
“Never Stop Learning and Growing.”
~ Kimberlee Slavik, Author of Memoirs of An Angry Sales Pro – Sales Leadership MUST change!

PROPOSED SOLUTION –

Do you currently offer training to help employees build stronger business acumen? This is another thing I really appreciated about working for Mark Hurd. We had a leadership summit and we were taught things like how we maintained a high credit rating and how it financially impacted our interest rates. He explained the difference in our ratings when we paid Net 30 versus Net 90. He explained that this is why it was important that we identified "preferred vendors" because not many companies could sustain a payment in Net 90. There were many other things that were taught about China and the impact it made on our quarterly earnings when China adjusted their currency rates. The more educated your employees are, the more they can defend the company policies and the more loyal they become. I left the summit actually feeling important and trusted. It really made me feel good about the company, the leadership, and myself. It also made taking that 10% cut in pay a lot more logical to me. Do you offer quarterly Leadership Summits? I highly recommend them.

Mentor Tip for Fellow Sales Pros –
"If your company doesn't help you grow, their competitor will."
~ Kimberlee Slavik, Author of Memoirs of An Angry Sales Pro – Sales Leadership MUST change!

Companies that have a "sales is a necessary evil" culture are less likely to acknowledge the benefits of having a more open communication with the sales organization. However, cultures that view sales as the most important roles in the company will embrace this open communication concept.

Which culture are YOU?
Which culture do you work for?

Providing Training that improves business acumen and creates a business centric communication style would be a major step in the right direction.

CHAPTER 7 -
Ethics – There Must Be Consequences for Bad Behavior, Don't Enable Them!

I have been dreading this topic. However, I woke up this morning and couldn't wait to write this chapter. I'm not sure why. Perhaps it is because this one is actually going to be pretty therapeutic for me. I am about to share stories that only my husband knows and some of them, he didn't know about until recently. These are definitely topics that I could never share during a job interview when I was asked **"Why did you leave?"**

I do want to preface this chapter by clarifying that I have actually worked alongside some of the most ethical people in sales and I have worked alongside some of the most disgusting people I've ever known. I've left jobs because of what I was subjected to. I've left jobs because I was embarrassed and ashamed of the companies I represented, the people that were my leadership, and even some of my peers.

PROBLEM IDENTIFIED –
Sex belongs at home, not work. EVER.

The reason this chapter is so important is because it is a topic that has been a dirty little secret way too long. I sincerely hope my readers reach out to me with their perspectives and comments. What I want to know is if these stories are exclusive or pervasive to the sales world? It's so difficult for me to envision these behaviors happening in other corporate departments like Legal, Accounting, Shipping, or Information Technology (IT) but maybe I am naive.

Are all sales organizations full of stories of chronically bad behavior? Is this topic one of the main reasons sales has such a bad reputation? I have sold and participated in selling over two billion dollars of intangible offerings during my career and I have never had to leverage a room full of naked women to close any of those deals. I also am confident that I have never LOST a deal to a competitor due a room full of naked women as a competitive advantage. I've also never lost a deal because I refused a sexual advance or won a deal because I DID accept a sexual advance. Yet I have been surrounded by people that believed these actions were necessary to get a deal over the finish line.

With that said, I am sharing just a FEW stories describing different scenarios that I have been exposed to as I tried to grow as a professional and maintain my ethics and morals as a sales professional.

I worked for a company for just a few months. I got the job through a recruiter so I felt obligated to make this job work so the recruiter didn't have to refund the money if I left. Two things happened that shocked me so much that I packed up my things and walked out without a job and without even giving an official resignation. I think most people would have sued them but that is not in my DNA. I simply removed this company from my resume and I won't even mention the company name to my closest friends.

I reported to the Senior VP of Sales and he was there for many years before I was hired. I closed my first sale within the first month and during the morning sales meeting, he announced to the rest of the team that "Kimberlee broke her cherry this week!"

I was so stunned that I couldn't speak, move, or react. The rest of the team sat there quietly and politely congratulated me. It was a very awkward moment. This is a disgusting term and has no place in my life, especially the workplace. And yet, this was one of the milder things I witnessed during my brief tenure at this company.

The offices were actually very nice. We had individual offices with walls and doors so they were very private. My office was next to the Senior VP so we shared a wall between us. One day, I was in my office and could hear very clearly him having sex in his office. I didn't know what to do. Do I leave? I was shocked. I packed things up and decided to go to lunch and as I was leaving he opened his door and said good-bye to his companion. She never looked at me. I only saw her from behind as she walked out of our office. He then asked me to come into his office and I said I was on my way out. He quickly caught on that his office might not be the best place to talk due to the activities that had just taken place. So he continued with, "Ok then. Can I speak with you in your office for just a minute because I actually need you to stay?"

I was very uncomfortable and frankly, I was a little scared too. He then proceeded to tell me that the companion was not his wife and his wife just called and was on her way to the office to meet me. He asked me to stay so he could introduce us and he added for me to not mention the other woman that had been in the office. He left to go to the bathroom and I gathered my things and never came back.

I did actually call a couple of my coworkers to say good bye and to thank them for their help and support and they confirmed that he was a known womanizer which is why his wife wanted to meet me. I was told that it was a running joke at the highest levels in the company what a pig this man was. Why was he allowed to stay? Was it because he was hitting his numbers? Because I can tell you that he made ZERO contributions to my sales success while I was there.

A very senior HR person once told me that when a man in the workplace harasses a woman, SHE becomes the liability, not the man because SHE can sue the company, not the man creating the uncomfortable work environment.

Because of this insight from an HR Executive, I have always simply left quietly without making any type of disruption or causing any gossip. The “Me Too” movement is changing things rapidly but I am skeptical that it is going to make a difference. As a mother of a young adult son, I also worry that this Me-Too movement is similar to the Salem Witch Trials. I fear it will trigger rampant false allegations towards men. Therefore, I couldn’t write a book about what is broken without including this uncomfortable topic.

The most disappointing thing that happened to me was with a CEO that I respected very much. He was like family to me. Even my husband adored him because they met on numerous Sales Achievement Club Trips.

One day this CEO and I were traveling for a conference together, when he told me he had a meeting area in his room and he invited me to come strategize on a huge transaction I was closing. I was honored to have that time with him and get his coaching!

Imagine my shock and disappointment when he made a move on me at his conference table. This man is beloved by all! He is funny and smart and dynamic and was a huge supporter of my early career. I worked for him for years and was very happy there. But when he made his move, my natural reaction was to push him so hard, I knocked him to the ground.

I was mortified but all he did was laugh and act like nothing happened and we immediately got back to work. It actually took me a few days for what happened to sink in. This was a man I respected and adored. I've been told that men think that when they make a pass at a woman, that she should feel it is a huge compliment. This could not be further from the truth. His behavior actually destroyed my respect for him. I felt dirty and was actually insulted that he thought I would be receptive to his advances.

For over five years, I admired him for being a good family man that loved his wife and children. So I was heartbroken that he shattered that image. I also really liked his wife and met her on those same achievement club trips that my husband attended. I felt so bad for her and her children because every smart woman knows that when a man makes a move, it doesn't mean that you are special; it means if he did it with you, then there have been others. So you aren't the first or the last one that he will attempt that with. It made me feel cheap and disrespected but I didn't tell my husband until recently because I didn't want him to be disappointed in him either.

I resigned shortly after the incident because I could never respect or trust him ever again and honestly, I feared retribution for resisting his advance. This was over 15 years ago and because of the Me-Too movement, suddenly women feel free to share stories like this one with each other. It's because of this new open communications that I recently learned about other women that had the same experience as me. We all had one major thing in common - None of us reported him because we didn't want to hurt him or his family. Even with the Me-Too movement, the women that compared notes with me all agree that we would prefer to continue to keep quiet in order to protect him; he is THAT likable!

As we all know, it takes two to tango. These are just two examples of men misbehaving but let me tell you that women are also a huge part of the problem. My first software sales job was a pretty intense culture. There were motivational signs hanging up that said, "Second Place is the First of the Losers." One of my peers came back from a lunch meeting and she was openly bragging that she was for sure going to close her deal because she slept with the customer during lunch and because he was married, she was confident that he now HAD to sign the deal. She bragged about this so casually as if she was describing what they ate for lunch. She was PROUD that she now had their affair to hold over his head. Because she was so verbal, everybody in the office was aware of her activities during lunch, including management. She was actually celebrated for her conviction to do whatever it took to get the deal done and worked there several years after I left.

The one thing that each of these stories share is that the unethical behaviors were known by all and at very high levels within each company and the perpetrators were ENABLED, often at the highest levels within each company. There were no consequences for these behaviors. So these bad behaviors were covered up, ignored, celebrated, embraced, and even joked about.

I have dozens of stories on this topic including drugging unsuspecting business women, but that is as far as I am going to go with the topic of sex. I want to continue this chapter by sharing some other questionable ethical behaviors that are fairly common before I start offering potential solutions.

Aren't Unethical Ethics better than no Ethics at all?

**PROBLEM IDENTIFIED –
KICK BACKS are alive and well**

Another company that I worked for had a manager with pretty open ethics issues. He even consulted with each of us individually (he must not have known we all compared notes) asking for our opinion. He said that a Partner had offered to pay him a percentage of whatever our team referred to them. From our group discussions, we all told him adamantly that this was unethical. But just the fact he consulted each of us over this matter, shattered our trust in him and made us assume he did it anyway.

Another time, our team was told to use a specific partner exclusively moving forward. We had already established trust and relationships with our own partners but this was an order. I later learned from one of the partner's employees that they had sent a limo and took our sales manager to several Gentlemen's Clubs the night before this requirement was given to us. This partner was not the best one. But we had no choice but to follow the direction of our leader and use them. Was it in the best interest of our clients? No. Was it in the best interest of our company? No. The only person that benefited from this mandate was our leader.

I know for a fact that I lost deals early in my career due to kickbacks. I used to sell miscellaneous data center items such as tapes, racks, furniture and anything else clients wanted to buy. I kept losing to a competitor that sold the exact same things as I did but they were about 40% more expensive. One of my clients told me that he was buying from them because after he spent a certain amount of money with them, he got a trip to Germany and gift cards so he had spending money once he was there. It's one thing to try and overcome a competitor's sales tactics, it's another thing to overcome a client's unethical behavior. I walked away from that business. It wasn't worth it.

PROPOSED SOLUTION –

Why should an employee report any misbehaviors? What are bad behaviors costing the company? What would it be worth to avoid potential law suits? I encourage a reward system for employees that expose suspected inappropriate actions and employees should be allowed to submit their suspicions anonymously. After a discreet investigation was completed, and bad behavior was proven, THEN the employee could have an opportunity to reveal who they are so they can receive their reward. Many may prefer to remain anonymous because their reward was seeing justice served.

PROBLEM IDENTIFIED – DIVIDE AND CONQUER is a destructive leadership tactic

I've had managers that played a very destructive game with our team called, "Divide and Conquer." During one-on-ones, one of these managers would tell us that other members on our team didn't like us. He would get pretty personal regarding our personalities and why others didn't like us. I would leave his office wondering what was his agenda? Did he want to make sure we never compared notes? Did he want to make sure we didn't help each other? I still don't understand what this man had to gain by constantly trying to create friction within our team. But this game of divide and conquer happens between peers, managers, clients, and competitors.

The final story I will share, led to another of my departures from another really successful sales role. Any salesperson that has been required to present a QBR (Quarterly Business Review) knows that they are intended for sales to "try out" for their jobs. During your presentation, you are expected to review the previous quarter and forecast the forthcoming quarter. If these back-to-back quarters describe missed quotas, your job security would become in jeopardy and the best-case scenario would be that you will most definitely be micromanaged to ensure that your sales results got back on track.

At this particular company, we would get newly formatted presentation decks just a day or so before we were expected to present in front of about 30 of our peers and sales teams. Most of us pulled all-nighters to get the decks presentable so we were exhausted and stressed the day we presented. As I was plugging my laptop into the projector, my sales manager suddenly asked me, "Kim, is it true that your husband gets up every morning at 3am so he is at his office by 4am each day?" I was confused why he was asking me this and I had my presentation on my mind so I quickly answered, "Yes." He then asked a follow-up question, "And what time does he get home each night?" Again, I did not understand this line of questioning or why it was happening before my QBR. I answered, "Around 7pm." He then burst out laughing and loudly stated, "And you actually think he is WORKING?!"

This company and its people are ruthless but you could hear an audible gasp from the audience. I was too shocked to react so I proceeded with my presentation. Immediately afterwards, three different people came up to me and told me that if I didn't go to HR, they would. I begged them not to do that. Yet my phone rang within the hour. It was HR.

I will continue this story in the next chapter about HRs role. But one thing was for sure; my husband wouldn't be attending any future company parties thrown by this man after I told him what he said. So I instantly knew I was done here.

Why are the various behaviors I have described in this chapter acceptable? Why is this still happening in 2019? Today I am old and fat so nobody makes moves on me anymore. But every young woman I've mentored has eventually asked for coaching after being harassed in the same ways. Two young women have even text me for advice WHILE men in leadership roles were aggressively pursuing them while traveling. The conclusion I've come to is that the women that actually accept and participate in these behaviors are the reason that it continues. And these women are also why those of us that just want to do a good job and be respected by the men they work with, have to endure advances. It must be confusing for men when some women are game and others are not. If men knew that none of the women wanted to play those games, they would be less likely to even try.
Right? Perhaps if they knew there would be other consequences, they would stop. Right?

I know that in our country, we are innocent until proven guilty. The fact that these types of behaviors are difficult to prove adds to the complexity of addressing the problems and a huge reason that women don't file charges. But multiple people knew about the behaviors I just described, and executives knew they were happening. Why were these men allowed to continue in leadership roles? If one of them had been accused of shooting someone, they would be terminated without a doubt. There must be a zero tolerance for these other types of behaviors in the workplace as well – for BOTH men and women.

Sadly, the few stories I just shared were not even the worst things I have experienced. Some things I have been subjected to are too graphic to put in this book. I chose the stories I shared because despite excellent sale performance, I ended up leaving several great sales positions because of unethical behaviors. How much did my resignations cost these companies? And what about all the women that actually **sued** over these types of behaviors?

I used to think that leaving quietly was the right thing to do for all concerned. But I think the silence is part of the reason why it continues to be a problem. **There has to be consequences to cause change.**

PROBLEM IDENTIFIED – BAD BEHAVIOR IS EXPENSIVE -

Here is a great article on the subject.
https://www.marketwatch.com/story/as-harvey-weinstein-takes-a-leave-of-absence-heres-how-much-sexual-harassment-costs-companies-and-victims-2017-10-07

This article talks about how difficult it is to calculate how much this is actually costing corporations. It explains how companies would rather pay to "get rid of the problem" than to terminate the perpetrator. It also mentioned that sexual harassment complaints have remained steady since 1992. But they admit that they only track the ones reported. Nobody knows how many incidents (like mine) are never reported or how many are quietly paid off to avoid documentation of the offense. I can tell you that this chapter subject is the number one topic when I am mentoring young women AND men today. Their concerns today are not very different from they were when I was their age.

I also refuse to connect on LinkedIn with men that exhibit these types of behaviors because I don't want for even one person to see our mutual connections and think, "I wonder if she..." Although I won't connect with them, I do keep a close eye on where they currently work and it effects my perception of that company! If they would hire someone like these men, I tend to judge the company as one for which I would never want to work. I'm sure I'm not the only person that thinks that way.

I need to withdraw my application for employment. You just hired the reason I quit!

I also read a lot about companies on Glassdoor. And while I know that companies pay Glassdoor to improve their online reviews, I do tend to go read the negative comments before I consider a job offer to see what types of complaints are out there. Does anybody complain about not being paid? Do they complain about discrimination? What do they say about leadership?

How much does this cost a company in recruiting top talent? I just don't understand why it's tolerated when bad behavior obviously comes at a pretty hefty cost.

PROPOSED SOLUTION -
This is the one and only chapter for which I have no passionate, proposed solution. Instead, I have several proposals for consideration.

There was a time that companies had strict "no fraternizing policies" in place. Coworkers could not date. And if a couple got married, one of them would be forced to resign. This may sound prehistoric today but it makes total sense. And I worry about the "Me Too" movement and how it could affect young men like my son. I've asked him about dating women at work and he is adamant that he will never "dip his pen in the company ink" because it is way too risky. He also worries about retaliation and false accusations if a relationship dissolves. I hope all young people think this way but it is highly doubtful so perhaps companies could help educate them by putting policies in place to discourage fraternizing.

Almost every place I've worked, I've had to take an online course on ethics. But they focused a lot on not sharing trade secrets, not interpersonal relationships in the office. I think it would be wise to crank this type of training up.

People don't seem to be concerned about losing their job but they would be concerned about losing something they have invested a lot of time in achieving such as their credentials. If a Doctor did something to a patient that was inappropriate, he or she could lose his/her license to practice medicine. The same thing applies to Attorneys and other licensed practitioners.

If certifications became the norm...
If certifications became desired and credible...
If an MSL (Master of Sales Leadership) was difficult to obtain... If sales leadership certifications were prestigious...
Perhaps people would fear losing these credentials they worked so hard to achieve. Then (maybe) these behaviors I described would be less likely to take place.
If workplaces worked with HR to establish a no tolerance policy for these behaviors and people knew they would lose their jobs, perhaps these behaviors would stop or at least decrease significantly.

One thing is for sure - Without consequences, nothing is EVER going to change!

I look forward to what YOU have to say about this chapter!

CHAPTER 8 – Human Resource's Role – Sales is NOT the Enemy, We Are Your CUSTOMER!

PROBLEM IDENTIFIED –
HR's role is to protect the COMPANY, not the EMPLOYEE.

When I started my career, HR's role in each employee's life was a very important part of the employee/employer relationship. HR lured top talent by offering the best benefits, pensions, tuition reimbursement, and much more. HR was there to ensure employees were happy, safe, and healthy. Everybody LOVED HR!

Today, HR's relationship with employees is very different. HR's main focus is on protecting the COMPANY, which is why I mentioned that I would continue the QBR story during this chapter.

I have observed extremely successful women report misconduct to HR. And then suspiciously lose their job based upon "poor performance." And if that weren't bad enough, it appeared they became blackballed and unable to find work. There was a storage company that was notorious for their blatant sexist behaviors yet I never saw a woman, that filed a formal complaint, leave that company unscathed. In *Visnostic Sales and Marketing*, I explain the psychology behind "You Are Who You Are Because of Where You Were When." And it's because of what I have observed, that I have established a "walk away quietly policy" when I was exposed to any misconduct during my career.

Therefore, when I received that call from HR about what occurred during my presentation, I immediately asked that they document that I was not the one that contacted HR. I wanted it noted in my personnel file that I did not instigate this discussion. I wanted it put in writing that HR contacted ME.

I also felt compelled to reassure them that I have never sued and will never sue any company that I work for. I told them that I loved my job and if I was offended, I would quietly leave. As I type this, I realize I sound like a coward. And I can't deny that. HR notified me that they were going to open a formal investigation into my manager's behavior and they would be checking back with me. They wanted names of people that might have witnessed him acting inappropriately and I told HR that I didn't want to contribute to the investigation.

I want to reiterate that I was 199% of my quota within the first six months I worked there and was awarded a Sales Club Trip that included only the top 3% of the salespeople in the company. And while my quota exploded the second year, I grew my business over

60% YoY. I was not failing and I was making an extremely good income. Yet, just weeks after this call from HR, I was put on a performance improvement plan. These tactics are done to build a case against the person that has been mistreated in order to prepare for any potential lawsuits.

Once again, I resigned before I had another job because I now had so much "noise" in my head, I knew I could no longer be effective. I no longer WANTED to work for a company that treated a victim (their term, not mine) like this.

Why would any good company take any of its top producers and put them through any psychological abuse like this?

PROPOSED SOLUTION -

How do we fix it? With lawsuits rampant, I don't think there is an answer to this question. Too many employees look at these scenarios as their own potential "Lottery Win" so companies have to take drastic measures to protect themselves. Because I'm a businesswoman, I understand the logic in this behavior but that doesn't mean it is right or should be an acceptable practice.

I think the best way to start working towards change is to acknowledge the reality behind HRs role and start strategizing on how to balance company protection with employee protection. Are you really helping the right person or are you enabling the actual guilty person?

Another reason I am a huge proponent of mentoring is because I am fully aware that my stories and experiences through the years are not isolated incidences. Who can people trust to share their stories? A mentor is the safest confidant because I don't think HR is in a position today that allows them to help employees.

PROBLEM IDENTIFIED -
HR is a huge part of the problem with a company's perception of their Sales Organization.
HR is always involved in terminations and salespeople are considered disposable. HR often sees more salespeople resign or terminated than any other position in most companies. And when departments' personnel turn over, HR is impacted the most. However, HR's attitude is a direct result of leadership at the highest levels.

And let's get realistic for a moment. Everybody knows that a resignation is better for a company than a termination or layoff. I've seen people abused because sales leadership wanted them to resign. And I've seen some brutal behaviors including public humiliation and intimidation. And despite seeing multiple "investigations" conducted by HR around abuse claims, I have yet to see an abuser punished. Almost always, the accuser disappeared and those of us left behind always assumed there was some sort of settlement because the person that left refused to tell us what happened. This silence is typically part of the separation agreement.

HR is not much different than sales; their behavior is driven by the financial impact on the company. So technically, HR is working their plan and sometimes it causes bad behavior.

I've never been involved in a business lawsuit but I know dozens of people that DID sue their companies and while they never disclosed the details of their settlements, I have seen most of these people have a very difficult time finding work again. Several of them have indicated that they suspect that they have been blackballed. So if the details of the settlements are supposed to be confidential, how could they be blackballed? Is it just paranoia on their part or are the non-disclosure agreements being breached?

PROPOSED SOLUTION -

First of all, how is all this bad behavior even legal? Aren't there labor laws in place that protect employees from abuse? I don't know much about this because I would rather take the energy spent on a lawsuit and go do something constructive instead. There ARE good companies out there, they are just extremely difficult to find.

For HR to change the way Salespeople are viewed, HR has to be educated on the value the sales organization brings to a company. It would also be beneficial if HR would take a more proactive role in promoting the importance and significance of a successful sales organization. HR could also "police" the culture to remind leaders at the highest levels to only speak about sales with respect. Sales culture starts at the very top but even the best-intentioned leader can slip occasionally and verbalize frustration. HR can help mediate and remind how single every word said by a leader can impact a culture positively or negatively.

Few leaders take time to communicate the importance of the sales department's success to any employees, especially HR. I recommend that senior leaders hold regular meetings with HR to strategize how to retain salespeople, how to reward success, and how to recognize top performers. These meetings need to avoid negative discussions about sales and focus on replicating top performance with the bottom performers. Topics should include mentoring programs, leadership training, investments in sales training and other business education, team building, developing better sales tools, fractional sales leadership assessments, outside consulting services, and compensation enhancements.

Making time for these meetings will build a foundation for a positive sales culture that too few companies have today. There are other subtle things HR can do. For example, when I was hired at a Japanese company, honor and integrity were of utmost importance. When I received my new employee packet, it was actually customized for the sales organization. On the front of the folder said, "Sales Talent Acquisition." That may sound silly but I recall how good I felt when I opened the FedEx package and that was the first thing I saw.

Inspirational Quote –

"The most influential persuasion tool you have in your entire arsenal is your integrity."

~Zig Ziglar

Another little thing that I sincerely appreciated was coming to work on my first day and my office was decorated with welcome gifts and hand-written letters from each leader. I've also liked coming to work and having a nameplate at my desk. One company even had personality tests given to each employee before they started and the nameplate included their top five strengths. It was a great icebreaker and allowed people to identify areas in which they had in common with new hires. Every desk in every department had each employees name framed with their top five personality traits listed.

PROBLEM IDENTIFIED –

Using personality tests/preferred profiles to eliminate candidates does not work and is costing companies a lot of money!

This is such a lazy way to hire and I am grateful this fad is fading fast.

I interviewed for a software company that I LOVED! Had they hired me, I have no doubt, I would have been their top performer and would still be there today! I had been reselling their product for five years and was the top producer. I understood their software better than most of their current salespeople.

The sales manager at the time knew me well and she had already offered me the job. I was told I needed to take some sort of personality assessment just to complete the process but I was assured it was just a technicality. But per HR, the manager couldn't move forward with hiring me because the results of that personality test didn't fit their desired profile.

I not only could have hit the ground running, I brought a healthy pipeline with me. The person that they did hire didn't sell a thing and was terminated six months later.

PROPOSED SOLUTION –

Never make hiring decisions on these silly tests. There is no such thing as the perfect personality profile. You need diversity to have a strong team. Looking for the perfect profile is insane and will inhibit the collaboration and creative process that occurs when different personalities communicate and work together to solve business issues. Furthermore, just as compensation drives behavior, people will try and guess what they need to say to slant those personality tests.

PROBLEM IDENTIFIED –

Sales Training and onboarding are not enough to ensure sales success of new hires. Sadly, most companies have terrible sales onboarding as it is because the person putting the onboarding together has never been in sales.

PROPOSED SOLUTION –

Create a self-paced career advancement plan that includes sales leadership training for individual contributors. Educating individual contributors on sales leadership skills will also help them accept and understand their own management. But be sure that salespeople are involved in approval of the sales training content! I've taken sales training that was awful because the person that picked it out was not in sales.

PROBLEM IDENTIFIED –
There are no internship programs in place for salespeople or sales leadership.

PROPOSED SOLUTION –
Create both internal and external mentoring programs to promote career growth. Mentoring programs are another indicator that a company sees sales as an important role that deserves a clear career path to encourage retention of employees. (see chapter 5)

When I was at HP, one of my favorite things they did was identify new college graduates that would be on the management career track. These candidates were chosen because they stood out during the interview process and were immediately presented three profiles of executives for them to choose as a mentor. A young woman chose me and HR introduced us to each other and explained the formal mentoring program to us on a videoconference. HP had a program we followed and we became quite close. The day I left, and to my relief, she asked me to continue the mentoring relationship and ten years later, we are great friends. In fact, AFTER I left HP, the mentoring relationship actually got stronger because we were not restricted by the "rules" of the program. Plus, as I mentioned earlier, having a mentor outside of the company is extremely powerful.

Just having this type of program sends a strong message to the sales organization that they are important and their happiness and emotional health matters to the company. Mentoring can also fill that void by giving new employees someone to

The main point I hope this chapter drove home is to let HR know that WE know the games that are played. So instead of attempting to mask them, ignore them, or continue playing the game, let's work together to make things more productive for us all.

CHAPTER 9 –
Biological Facts – Discrimination is a Symptom of the REAL Problem

*The local business journal wants to do an article on the 10 most powerful women in our company.
How quickly can we hire 9 more women?*

**PROBLEM IDENTIFIED –
We are reluctant to acknowledge the benefits of our biological differences because we don't take time to understand them.**

What do you think of when you read "biological differences?" Gender? Age? Race? Sexual Preference? To ME, discrimination in any of these categories is actually a SYMPTOM of the REAL problem, which is that humans prefer to be with people that they have things in common. People want to relate to those around them. For example, consider clubs. Aren't they really just groups of people that have things in common? Don't people join clubs because the members enjoy the same things?

I believe that many men prefer to work with men because they can behave differently when a room is full of all men. I don't think all men are comfortable adapting their behavior when that "different" sex is in the room.

To my male readers, you may have a "fight or flight" instinct kick in and want to skip this chapter but I am begging you not to do that. Please read this even if you are the most supportive man on the planet. I want to give you a peak into what your wife, mother, daughter, or granddaughter may go through out in the professional world.

With that said, I am going to focus on sexism in this chapter because I've been personally impacted by it in both positive and negative ways. However, I am very aware that age discrimination is alive and well because I feel it more and more each year. Another discrimination that nobody talks about is called sizeism and it's actually legal in every state except Michigan. In fact, research shows weight discrimination has increased by 66 percent in the past decade and is, by some estimates, as prevalent as racial discrimination. The stigma of being fat follows Americans everywhere: at home, in medical settings, at school and at work, where discrimination is rampant — and perfectly legal and socially acceptable.

I also know that racism and other discriminatory attitudes are thriving despite efforts to extinguish them in the workplace. I'm hoping readers will share their personal stories with me so I can include those perspectives in future editions of this book. But for now, please realize that my stories are not really SEXISM problems.

ALL these stories are really about people that work together, are different from each other, and don't fully understand or respect those differences. People are most comfortable with people like themselves. Understanding this is the first step in managing it.

For example, I recently read an article that Corporate America made a huge mistake laying off people in their 50's because they now see a strong NEED for their work ethic and experience to help lead the Millennials and Generation-Zs in the business world. Suddenly, the differences that made the older people less desirable are exactly why they need them back in the workforce.

But misogyny is a strange thing. And I actually think the word is way too strong to properly describe what exists in the workplace today.

The definition of Misogyny by Wikipedia is:
Misogyny is the hatred of, contempt for, or prejudice against women or girls. Misogyny manifests in numerous ways, including social exclusion, sex discrimination, hostility, androcentrism, patriarchy, male privilege, belittling of women, disenfranchisement of women, violence against women, and sexual objectification.

While I am sure this blatant hatred exists. I can honestly say that I never felt HATED. I have felt misunderstood which has led to disrespect, underutilization, and other frustrations. I think we each (and I do mean EACH of us – me included) have our own subconscious discrimination hurdles to overcome. Here is a very innocent example:

Look at the business book collection you have in your current library. What are the names of some of the authors? Do you see a pattern? What do they all have in common?

Right before I published my first book, I was encouraged to use K. Slavik as my author name instead of Kimberlee Slavik so that it wasn't so obvious that a woman wrote the book. This suggestion shocked me but it also made me reflect on my own business book library; my authors include Mike Bosworth, Jim Collins, Tom Rath, Matt Dixon, Simon Sinek, Dale Carnegie, Napolean Hill, Tom Hopkins, Neil Rackham, just to name a few. To make things easy on you, check out this article written in 2019 listing the top 25 business books – https://www.businessinsider.com/best-selling-business-books-bill-gates-warren-buffett-2018-1

I realized that the only book I have in my library that was written by a woman is Sheryl Sandberg's *Lean In*. I suspect that your library looks very similar. Why do you think this is the case? Don't women write books? Don't readers think that women also have experience and have something important to say? Aren't most teachers women? So why wouldn't we tend to expect women to teach us better ways to sell, market, advertise, or be more successful in business? Where are all the best-selling books written by women?

One of the most difficult things about being in sales has been being a woman but also, one of the BEST things about being in sales was being a woman! So I have learned first-hand that any negative challenges that I experienced, were offset by the benefits that I experienced. This same observation applied to every woman that worked for me as well.

When I was interviewing during my 20's and 30's, I was consistently one of the final two candidates. Yet a man seemed to always end up getting the position I really wanted. The reason I love working with recruiters is that they actually can tell you the truth about why decisions are made. I was shocked and frustrated how many people admitted I was the better candidate but they couldn't risk me getting pregnant and going on maternity leave.

Because of this feedback, I ended up telling people during the interview that I knew there were things they were concerned about that they legally couldn't ask me so I wanted them to know that I wasn't having any children. I also made a point to never mention my son because I knew they would also be concerned that I would take off work when he was ill or had a school event.

As a Sales Leader, can you deny that you don't also have the same thoughts or concerns when you interview women?

Right or wrong, these biases are a valid reality and concern. I've had women work for me that were emotional wrecks because they were on fertility drugs. I hired one women four times and she was a nightmare to manage. She was constantly taking off work due to family emergencies. All of her emergencies were legitimate but why don't the men we hire have the same challenges? These constant emergencies had me in damage control mode more than I would have preferred. Yet all these challenges were worth it.

Why did I hire her four different times? Because despite the disruptions, when she was focused, she was the best salesperson I have ever seen in my entire career and I respected her for that. There are some talents that you just can't teach.

I admit that it would have been easier to hire someone else but I knew this Lady. I knew her strengths. I knew her integrity. I knew this woman would be my top performer. And she was EVERY. SINGLE. TIME. she worked for me!

Leaders have to figure out ways to work around our biological realities instead of avoiding them. It's pure laziness for a leader to hire a weaker candidate due to these types of biases.

Steve Jobs said
"A-Players hire A-Players, B- Players hire C-Players."
There is nothing in this Steve Jobs quote about men versus women.

Our biological differences are fact. It's life. I've worked for companies that believed women were the best candidates. And I've worked for companies that believed women were the worst candidates. They are both wrong!

I am adamant that all sales and sales leadership MUST be diversified! What is sad is that a lot of what I am going to write could end my career because these facts are taboo in Corporate America today. Isn't that crazy? You can have sex with a potential client at lunch and be praised for going that extra mile but I can mention the differences between men and women and get blackballed professionally because I may actually offend someone. THIS MUST CHANGE! So here we go...

Women are better at nurturing. I've seen men sell, close the deal, get their commission check, and move on. Women that have worked for me tend to kick into high gear AFTER the sale because they want to ensure their clients have a great post-sales experience. Women tend to actually care about their clients and have a natural instinct to nurture their clients. And clients LOVE to feel appreciated and cared for. Before you come after me with a pitchfork and a flaming torch, I am not saying this as a blanket statement. I am saying that IN GENERAL, women are better at this. But I HAVE seen men also very good at post-sales support; it just didn't seem as natural to me (as an observer and leader).

Men are better at bonding during activities. Most men I know love to golf with potential clients and men love to buy when vendors do things with them. Think about this – How many WOMEN take clients to Gentlemen's Clubs to close business? How many MEN take clients to these types of bars to close business? Women don't feel the need to DO things to bond; we tend to TALK to bond and I don't think a whole lot of talking goes on in Gentlemen's Clubs. Chances are that during a one-hour lunch, we can learn more about our clients than a man learns after an entire day on the golf course because we are naturally better at communicating.

As you can imagine, I have had opportunities to golf on some incredible courses. I've been to Pebble Beach. I've golfed in Carmel, South Beach, Palm Beach, Palm Springs, and Phoenician just to name a few. Yet I think golf is the biggest waste of time. During a Golf Tournament full of clients and/or potential clients, why would anybody want to spend an entire day with just three other people? **When we hosted or participated in scrambles or golf events, I would actually beg to drive the beverage cart!** That way, I could see everybody and when I drove up, people were really happy to see me because I had alcohol!

They loved telling me about their game and they loved asking me about how others were doing. I felt a stronger bond doing that with more people than being stuck with three people for an entire day. I still got to enjoy the course and views and I had a great time. But I also understand that not everybody thinks like me.

Now think about that for a moment...wouldn't it make strategic sense to have some salespeople golfing with their biggest opportunities AND having others driving the beer carts to ensure all the clients were exposed to your company? Doesn't it make sense to leverage the different preferences to our benefit? One is not right or wrong. They are different. And that is a very GOOD thing!

Men are different than women and THAT is also a very good thing. That may be a huge shocker for some of you reading this book. But it's basic biology. And we need to learn to respect and embrace our differences! The way to do this is to UNDERSTAND those differences! You really do need both men and women on every team and at every leadership level in order to benefit from these differences. For every negative women stereotype that you believe, there are equal numbers of negative traits that men have as well.

I was hired by a man that put together one of the best all-women teams I've ever seen. Sadly, he was demoted and a new leader was brought in and he met with his newly inherited team of women leaders. During his first meeting with us, he commented, "Women are nurturers by nature and do best in support roles." Obviously, I am not going to disagree about the nurturer comment but what I take issue with, is that he considered being a nurturer to mean that would make it impossible for women to be effective leaders! So I was stunned that he said the second part of his sentence. Obviously, HE was not a nurturer!

He then proceeded over the next four months, taking each woman out of her successful leadership role and replacing her with one of his male buddies. The women ended up in individual contributor roles such as training, internal communications, and other administrative roles with fancy titles. Each time he made one of these changes, he put out a mass communication announcing the "promotions." In fact, I still have a copy of the email he sent out about my "promotion" as well!

This insulted our intelligence. How is going from leading a team of 70 people to an individual "support" role (with no pay increase) a promotion? This was blatant sexism and he got away with it the entire time he was at that company. This has to stop!

Even his tactics were sexist in nature. I was managing a team of all men. He went behind my back to my managers and told them he was going to move me out. I was unaware of this action but I certainly felt the results of his secret conversation.

Suddenly, nobody was turning their reports into me and the men stopped attending our team meetings. The responses to my emails became extremely less urgent to them. So I could 'feel' something was seriously 'off' with the team.

And one day at a conference, I was speaking with one of my direct reports and told him that I knew what was about to happen. I was actually talking about a change that was coming in a different department. But HE thought I was talking about something else! He got so excited! He said, "I'm so relieved! I haven't been able to celebrate my new role with my wife yet! Thanks for letting me know you finally know I'm taking your job! What is your new role going to be?"

The look on my face must have let him know that this was news to me because the excitement faded from his face immediately. I was shocked. I asked him what he was talking about and he was mortified when he realized I wasn't referring to his replacement of me as the leader of our team.

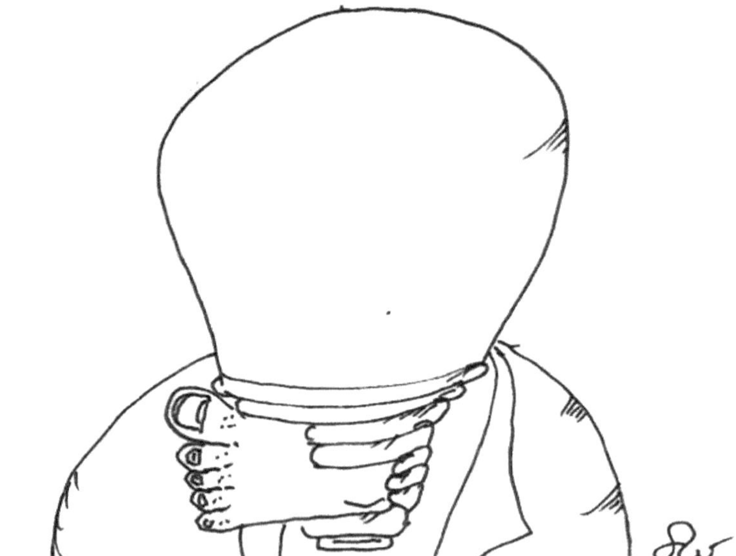

Foot in Mouth Syndrome

This uncomfortable situation obliterated everything I had accomplished along with the relationships I had worked so hard to build with my entire team. And I have zero respect for the man that came in and caused so much destruction. Yet what he did was completely acceptable by our company. His tactics were viewed as a chess game. He was just moving his pieces around to get what he wanted.

If his behaviors were just directed towards me, I would say that maybe I deserved to be taken out of the leadership role. However, there were SEVEN of us that had these same games played with our careers. SEVEN of us that had been showing major improvements in the businesses we were running. He was very sloppy at this game he was playing, yet it was effective. He single handedly got all of us moved out and his buddies moved in within just a few months. How can a man with these slanted views towards women, be allowed to stay in a leadership role and have the power to destroy successful women's careers?

One of the observations I have made during my career is that the men that respected me and supported me as my leaders had one major thing in common – their WIVES had very successful careers! In contrast, the men that played games with me and disrespected me each had wives that had more traditional roles. I also observed that one of these two groups of men were extremely loyal to their spouses and the other one was not. I'll let the readers guess which one did the cheating. I hope someone does some studies on this because this has been 98% predictable during MY career. All three of my favorite leaders - Ron, Gary, and Dave have incredibly strong wives that have extremely successful careers.

Because of the way some men have treated me professionally, I even make a point of asking about their spouses' careers during the interview process. I also invite men, including clients, to bring their wives when I host client dinners so that nobody misinterprets the intent of our meetings. Plus, I sincerely enjoy establishing relationships with the spouses of my clients and my co-workers. They tend to become some of my best advocates and friends because they are not accustomed to this type of respect from their spouses or other vendors.

There are stereotypes that teach us that men are more cerebral and women are way too emotional. However, I sure have seen a lot of emotional men during my 30-year sales career! In fact, as a leader, I get cursed at a LOT by MEN. Men get angry and hostile and everybody around them is expected to just sit there and let them express themselves in the manner in which they are most comfortable. One of these outbursts that I was enduring one day was a rant by a very senior level executive that was angry how long training took to get created, approved, and finally delivered.

Sexist Humor

Due to multiple large competitive losses, we needed some very specific competitive sales training ready within a week. However, our training department had a process that included legal review and approvals on all content before it could be released. I was told to make it happen FAST. In fact, my job was threatened if I didn't make it happen quickly.

So when I met with the woman that headed up training, I was told dozens of reasons why the training content could not and would not be ready and approved within the week requested. In fact, I was told it wouldn't be ready in a MONTH either. Now remember, I was cursed at over this earlier by a man. And my job was now on the line. So I got frustrated and told the training director that I wanted her to stop giving me excuses why it couldn't happen and to figure out a way to make it happen.

An hour later, I got a call from HR because she filed a complaint against me because I "raised my voice" at her.

Wow. I can tell you that double standards are alive and well in this world, both personally and professionally. I guarantee that if the same man that cursed at me had called her and cursed at her (which I did not), she would have never called HR and complained that he talked to her like that. It didn't even cross my mind to report him to HR.

We are so conditioned that women should behave one way and men should behave another way that I just don't think our society will ever change that viewpoint. So instead of changing our behaviors to accommodate the other person's needs, we should learn to embrace our differences and just accept them. If men think they have to change their behaviors to accommodate women, women will continue to be ignored and excluded unfairly.

There are even double standards in my own home; my husband and son will laugh and joke around and curse. But when I curse, my husband sings, "She's a lady..."

I'm not sure why you think we have a glass ceiling. This sign does the trick.

The reality is that both sexes have strengths and weaknesses.

Which is why our biological differences actually work quite well together when we focus on the positives of those differences.

We need to stop trying so hard to be politically correct and we need to embrace the reality of our differences. Even with the "Me Too" movement and all the allegations of misogyny recently, I still see an extremely unbalanced male/female ratio in leadership.

Despite California making it a law that all boards must have at least one woman, I still see all men boards. Why? What goes on in those board meetings that women cannot add value? (BTW, I'm actively looking to become a member of multiple boards, in case any readers out there are interested or have any recommendations.)

There are currently no women on the board but three of the men are pretty feminine.

I have actually been in meetings that discussed diversification numbers. During these meetings, we discussed the fact that the best candidates were not always hired because we had a "quota" to meet to ensure we had a specific percentage of races, sexual orientation, ages, and genders on board.

In fact, my husband was laid off early in his career because he was a white man in his 20's. They actually told him that despite having the best performance reviews, they couldn't afford to lay-off any of his (non-white) co-workers because the government was their biggest client and the government required a certain balance of diversity to keep their current contracts.

While this lay-off hurt our family, I completely understand and support the need for diversity in the workplace. However, I'm not sure setting quotas is the best way to manage it if good people are let go. If I were a minority, why should I work as hard if my job is protected?

Before I interview at a company, I look at their leadership website and when I see that women only have roles in training and HR, I won't bother talking with them. This screams to me that they have a sexist culture or at least they have a culture that "profiles" gender roles. How much is your own company's lack of diversity really costing you? How many very talented people are not interested in your current culture?

PROPOSED SOLUTION –

I know I threw out a lot of different things but that is what this chapter is about. We are all very different. We must learn about each other's differences. The only way we can respect each other is to educate each other on why and how those differences help us work better towards a common goal.

One of the best training I've ever received was called DiSC and it humbled me by helping me understand my own personality pros and cons. In addition, it helped me appreciate and respect the different personalities of family members, managers, peers, and clients.

But more importantly, once you understand all the different personalities around you, DiSC teaches how to adapt your own personality to be more compatible with your various environments. Sandler Sales Training calls this "mapping" to your audience. It's such an important understanding that I have used it almost every single day for the past 20+ years! I also credit it for helping sustain a 30+ year marriage.

DiSC or something similar to it, should be part of that sales leadership certification requirement that I proposed earlier in this book. And it should be mandatory for all leadership roles in every single company.

In fact, DiSC training is so important that I want to recommend a husband/wife team in Minnesota that teaches DiSC. They have done a beautiful job of tying Visnostics to their DiSC training. I highly recommend them if you are struggling with personality differences and/or challenges at your current company. They have also blended Visnostics into their training which makes it extremely powerful.

Their website is http://www.metamorphosiscct.com

We must accept the science behind our differences, embrace them, learn to respect them, and finally, we should learn to leverage these differences to make sales a better profession.

We can't make progress until we stop being fearful to discuss our differences. I also think the word, "discrimination" is thrown around way too much and some behaviors are incorrectly labeled as discriminatory, when in fact, it's something completely innocent.

We need to stop labeling everything as unfair or as some sort of discrimination. Instead, we should learn to better understand and manage our natural desire to be with people that we have things in common. This natural desire is often mislabeled as some sort of hateful behavior. We will only overcome this misunderstanding through education and practice.

As shocking as it may be to my readers, I don't actually think I was removed from my leadership role because I was a woman and the new VP hated women. I believe I was removed because the man is **terrified** of women because he doesn't understand them. I think he has been taught that there is power in building a "boys club." I believe he was determined to surround himself with people that he understood. And when you feel that you understand someone, trust is a natural outcome. I think he wanted to ensure he had people on his team that would embrace, support, and encourage each other. And he submitted to his natural instinct and surrounded himself with people like himself, which just happened to be all MEN. Is that sexism? Well, that is what society labels it. But I think it is based much more on our primitive instincts than hatred.

I highly recommend that all companies put more emphasis on diversity training. But let's not just learn to be politically correct because that isn't working; it tends to keep people from sharing their true thoughts and feelings. Let's find training that will help us understand our biological strengths. Let's have regular team building exercises to make those relationships stronger so we can learn to respect, accept, and even admire our differences so we can leverage those differences to be the best company and teammates we can be.

However, if a man thinks women shouldn't be in leadership roles because they are nurturers and therefore belong in support roles, that man should no longer be in a leadership role. And if women can't handle men talking like men without being offended, they need to also get out of leadership roles. If we are going to be successful, we must find a way to work together. If 50% of marriages can thrive despite these differences, I believe leadership teams can have much better percentages of success.

CHAPTER 10 -
Hire the Right Salespeople –
Make Us Proud to Work With Our Peers!

Your resume was full of lies. You'll fit in great here. Welcome to sales.

PROBLEM IDENTIFIED -
Bad behavior is contagious and toxic.

My first sales leadership role was when I was very young and I joined a company that had three partners. The partners had three very different personalities and they didn't agree on much. When they hired me, they set me down and let me know that we had a sales team in another state and they wanted me to advise them if they should keep the office open or close it.

I was introduced to the team via conference call and then I called each one individually. They sounded very "Eddie Haskell" to me. And by that, I mean they sounded extremely polite yet very insincere at the same time. I attempted to fly out to meet them and they had constant excuses that they were with clients and way too busy to meet with me.

With the Partners' blessings, I headed to their state anyway, office keys in hand, for a surprise visit. When I arrived, the office was locked up and was extremely tidy. I worked from the office all day. I called the guys and they each said they were with clients. One even said he was at the office with a client. I was at the office so I knew he was lying. I told him great because I was on my way to the office and couldn't wait to meet the client. It was dead silence on the other end of the phone. He ended up showing up in golf attire, a suntan, and he smelled like he had been outside. He knew he was busted for lying to me and sat me down and vented about how awful the company was. I fired him on the spot and took his laptop and files before he could do anything to them.

We compared his forecasts with his emails and uncovered even more lies. He must have warned the other two guys because they showed up and we basically went through the same things. What we uncovered was that these guys lived off their base salaries and golfed all day long. They were disgruntled and felt justified in their behavior because they didn't like the owners. One of the guys was actually a good man. But the others had way too much influence on him and he joined them in their bad behaviors.

When I got back to the corporate office, the partners sat me down and admitted they knew they had a problem with one of the guys but they never knew the negative attitude had spread in the office. That is the thing about keeping a bad person with a bad attitude. No matter how nice people are in the office, toxic behavior is contagious and negativity tends to be destructive.

You obviously have heard about his toxic personality.

PROPOSED SOLUTION –

When you see a cancer, cut it out before it spreads. **But (THIS IS VERY IMPORTANT!) before you do it, be sure you confirm the situation.** Too many times, I've seen managers eager to make an impression and prove they can make tough business decisions so they start shooting the staff. As a Sales Pro that has had multiple leaders fired and replaced, we go through the same dance with each of their replacements. These new leaders act like your buddy but we all know we are being evaluated and decisions are being made if we get to keep our job or if the new guy can bring in his own people. These people are NOT good leaders and they are very COSTLY leaders! It's going to take a much longer time ramping new people up, than improving an existing team!

That means that replacing salespeople will COST more than doing your job as a leader by FIXING WHAT IS BROKEN!

Before terminations take place, it is imperative that a good leader considers if he or she actually has the leadership skills that can turn the team around. Sadly, this is extremely rare in today's sales leadership. This MUST change because many terminations I've witnessed have been due to an incompetent LEADER versus an incompetent sales organization.

PROBLEM IDENTIFIED – Many employees leave because leaders don't view employees' CAREERS with the proper amount of respect they deserve.

"You are your own corporation!" It's ok to FIRE your employer!

Inspirational Quote –

You are the CEO of your life.

Hire, fire, and promote accordingly

After a decade of being in VP of Sales Roles, I accepted a role way beneath my capabilities but I did it because I was excited about the culture and the way the company treated me during the interview process. I also liked that I would be reporting directly to the CEO. So despite the lack luster title, I really liked my placement on the Org Chart. However, instead of including me with the senior level executives, I was grouped with Director level people. Some were outstanding but others were incompetent and even unethical. And worse yet – POLITICIANS! Yikes.

One of these people that were considered to be my peer was taking opportunities created by members of my sales team and changing them to be in his teams' pipeline. The first time I caught it, I assumed it was a mistake. The second time, I assumed he was incompetent. The third time, we had a serious discussion and he played dumb. The fourth time, he got very defensive. It became crystal clear that this was a man that had never been in a sales role and he was drunk with the dream of success. He desperately needed to show the executives how much he was growing the pipeline and he didn't care who he hurt to get his reports to look impressive. In fact, the more I worked with this man, the creepier he behaved. Hello? Why can't anybody see what I see? **The ENC Syndrome was rampant at this company.**

Mentor Tip for Fellow Sales Pros –
"Never Settle for Less Than You Deserve"
~ Kimberlee Slavik, Author of Memoirs of An Angry Sales Pro – Sales Leadership MUST change!

In addition to this unacceptable behavior with our CRM system, he also had an unusual obsession with age. He constantly referred to his teams age and to even my age. I warned him multiple times that he was going to get the company sued with his constant comparisons of peoples' capabilities with their ages. Furthermore, he spoke on my behalf and kept putting words in my mouth – with me standing right there! Everything this man did screamed how inexperienced his was.

After multiple attempts at resolving multiple issues with this creepy man, I actually went to the CEO and told him what was being done and warned him to not believe the pipeline reports. I also suggested that he limited my coworkers CRM permissions so he could no longer convert our opportunities to his team's opportunities. The CEO looked at me with a blank expression because he thought this guy hung the moon.

In fact, this guy ended up getting promoted to my level and this was a huge insult to me in every way. I actually should have resigned that day because I lost respect for leadership for making that decision AND I lost respect for MYSELF because leadership considered him to be my peer!

However, I attempted to convince myself that this must be a personal flaw of mine and I needed to not be so arrogant and cocky. I later observed other questionable behaviors such as fights with people at company events and lies about random things. Why would I continue to work for a company that believed that he and I were on the same level? Being insulted is one thing, but I also felt wildly disrespected. Making this person my peer, demonstrated to me that leadership did not appreciate my entire career and all of my accomplishments. I was ashamed to be working with this person and I became ashamed of the company for not seeing what I saw. The **ENC Syndrome** strikes again.

When employees don't see that the company appreciates the value they bring to a company, they will (and SHOULD) leave. And that is exactly what I did. I did feel vindicated because just a few months after I resigned, he was terminated for many of the reasons I mentioned above. The executives finally saw what I saw but it was too late. Why do companies seem to trust and support the wrong employees?

Mentor Tip for Fellow Sales Pros –
"Do Not Allow Anybody To Disrespect You."
~ Kimberlee Slavik, Author of Memoirs of An Angry Sales Pro – Sales Leadership MUST change!

PROPOSED SOLUTION -

To ME, everything I am about to suggest is common sense. But if that were the case, why is this subject even part of this book?! So here goes…

First of all, be careful when giving out promotions. These decisions are a huge reflection on leadership's core competency. Promoting the wrong people can destroy employee morale and can damage employee respect for the leaders in the company. It will also impact how employees feel about themselves. Furthermore, when incompetence or inexperience is rewarded when it's not deserved, it creates "noise" and questions around interoffice politics.

When employees see undeserving people recognized, it devalues any recognition they have received in the past and diminishes the value of any recognition received in the future.

If you want a first-class organization, hire first class people. Hire people with a proven track record, with an education, with morals, integrity, and gratitude. Hire a diverse team but don't just stick them together and expect them to take time to understand each other. Give them proper training. Have regular QUALITY team building exercises.

One company I worked for was located in a small town and their excuse for their hiring challenges was their location. Solution – open another office near a better talent pool! Trust me, it's costing you more money to NOT do this!

Never do anything to make them distrust each other. Incent them to work together. Create mentorship programs that encourage the experienced sales professionals to help new hires or younger employees. If you do all these things, each member of your team will feel RESPECTED.

When people feel respected, magic happens.

Once you know someone is doing something unethical or immoral, eliminate him or her immediately before resentment festers and respect is lost. As you've read, I've left multiple jobs after perceiving that leadership endorsed bad behaviors. Why would I want to jeopardize my own reputation by being associated with a company that allowed these behaviors and even promoted people that didn't deserve it?

If I viewed my career as my own little corporation, why would I stay and continue to work for a company that promotes substandard performers?

A promotion should never be given in order to inspire an employee; an employee MUST earn it. And the perception that the promotion was earned must not be solely the perception of the leadership team; it should also be the perception of his or her peers!

Mentor Tip for Fellow Sales Pros –
"Nobody Can Take Away Your Reputation. Protect It."
~ Kimberlee Slavik, Author of Memoirs of An Angry Sales Pro – Sales Leadership MUST change!

CHAPTER 11 – Technology is Destroying Sales. Do You Want Salespeople Selling or Inputing Data For Your Reports?

Be sure to update the CRM with data about the prospects that you don't have time to visit because you have to update the CRM.
THAT'D BE GREAT

It is ironic that while I was writing this chapter, Salesforce announced the acquisition of Tableau for $15.7 BILLION in stocks. Readers of *Visnostic Sales and Marketing* may remember that I am a huge fan of Tableau analytics and of course visualizations. So now the top CRM and the Top Analytics Companies have merged and life is about to improve – For EXECUTIVES and their love for reports!

What else do you think is about to happen? Of course Salesforce's

CRM reporting is about to get even better! So there has never been a more urgent need to get this problem acknowledged and addressed; **due to our obsession with reporting, we are distracting salespeople from selling by forcing them into data entry roles.**

When I started my sales career, we didn't have internet, cell phones, email, or social media; we had regular PHONES! Our most valuable sales prospecting tool were these very popular and expensive sheets of paper that were put into binders, called "Computer Intelligence Reports." They were also called "Market Intelligence Reports." They contained summaries of companies, their financials, and contacts. By the time our companies purchased them and circulated them to the sales teams, they were already outdated but it's all we had to prospect. We used them as we made calls and we wrote in them with any updates we gathered during the call. There were no reports. Our sales managers would ask to see our binders occasionally to read our notes and ensure we were making the required number of calls each week.

I recall purchasing my first CRM (Customer Relationship Management) software out of my own pocket. It was called ACT! And it set me back about $300. I would use the binders and the information to hand type in my contact information and call notes. I would also attempt to find out spouse information, children, pets, anniversaries, and birthdays. I eventually built a database of over 10,000 contacts and it was my most treasured possession as a sales professional. If you ever heard of people landing sales roles because of their "rolodex," this is a more modern version of that. During interviews, I bragged about my database. My database was in high demand. When I left a company, they got to keep my folders and business cards but I walked away with my database!

Then my biggest nightmare occurred; COMPANY OWNED CRM software was invented and embraced by almost every company over night. Suddenly, I was required to input, but unable to keep, contact information. For a few years, I actually attempted to maintain my personal database as well as my company's required database. Eventually it was too much and I accepted that my contacts were now the property of the companies for which I worked and I no longer took that information with me when I left.

CRM software was great for companies and not so great for salespeople. But then LinkedIn was invented and I started collecting my own data again by linking with as many clients as possible. This is how I continue to personally manage my client contacts today.

This has been an incredible evolution but it's reaching a point today that is not as positive as it began and here is why: As technology matures, it becomes more robust. And some of the biggest enhancements are with reporting. And management LOVES reports! I completely understand this. However, in order to run all those beautiful reports, someone has to input the data. Today, sales organizations are required to spend HOURS (not an exaggeration!) just to record an opportunity! There are way too many fields now and many CRM Admins think it's a smart idea to make many of those fields "mandatory" before an opportunity can be saved and demonstrate a healthy pipeline report.

Here is the reality of what ends up happening;

Most salespeople are in sales because they are NOT conventional office personalities, and most of the salespeople I know are actually administrative nightmares. I'm guilty as well. A great example is that I hate doing expense reports. I've been known to turn in six months of expenses at one time. I know how dumb this is. I know I am giving an interest free loan to my company when I delay getting reimbursed. Yet I still procrastinate because it's so administrative in nature! I want to be SELLING or doing strategic account planning. I do NOT want to be inputting phone numbers and addresses into someone else's database. This is costing us BOTH money!

So what do you think salespeople do when they have mandatory fields to fill out asking information they haven't gathered yet? They fill out bogus information so they can save the opportunity in their CRM!

Have you heard the term, "Trash In/Trash Out?" What is the point in all that robust reporting when the data entry is being forced on people that don't like doing it? The results are that the reports are rubbish AND the more administrative work forced on a sales organization, the less time they have to sell, which means there are fewer things to put into the CRM tool!

- Do you want administrators or do you want salespeople?
- Do you want them spending half of their day in front of their laptops or in front of clients?

So far, the solution I've observed from the executive level is to have sales leadership manage the input; If salespeople don't input everything into the CRM, their solution is to fire the sales leader!

NO! Not only will this turn the sales leader into an awful MANAGER (This is not Leadership!), now this sales leader will be turned into something so counterproductive that every employee in sales will suffer.

Remember when sales leadership was in place to help strategize, plan client meetings, and help their teams close sales?

During the last EIGHT years of my sales career, executives have sat in their office on conference calls going over numbers instead of getting engaged with salespeople and helping to close business. In fact, in the past eight years, I have had ONE leader go on TWO calls with me. And neither time, did he even add any value. He wasn't a sales leader; he was an administrator!

So now sales**people** AND sales **leadership** are both focused on data entry. Well, there won't be much data entry because there won't be much to input!

So as you can see, we have created a complex infrastructure full of time consuming administrative work in order to simplify the sales process.

PROPOSED SOLUTION – LET US SELL!

SIMPLIFY! KISS = Keep It Simple Stupid. Please don't take extroverted people that are gifted with their interpersonal skills and force them to do work intended for introverted and shy people! If these reports are so critical to making business decisions or reporting accurately to Wall

Street, hire an administrator to do this work. Have a weekly forecast call to review what was accomplished and have the administrator fill out CRM during the call.

I worked for a company that mandated over 30 fields in the CRM system that had to be filled out just to submit a new opportunity! THEN sales had to fill out a daily activity report and a report of what they would be doing in the future! If CRMs are so powerful, wouldn't the CRM produce reports that summarize the activities? The answer is YES. This same company had executives comparing the CRM reports with the daily reports created by sales as a way to validate the accuracy of what had been inputted into the CRM. STOP THIS INSANITY.

"Analysis Paralysis" does not belong in sales!

Mentor Tip for Fellow Sales Leaders -
NO ANALYSIS PARALYSIS
You hired Salespeople. Don't turn them into Administrators!

Technology is a great thing. I would much rather have CRM software than those binders. But there are companies I've left because the expectations were unreasonable and nobody respected sales enough to take time to walk in the shoes of salespeople. When was the last time executives at your company spent a day with salespeople to see exactly what is being forced upon the organization?

Sales organizations are not a necessary evil. Treat sales as a valued organization and you will watch people behave as a valued organization. Treat them like a punching bag and watch them leave and watch revenues fall short. Treat them like data entry clerks and watch a mess beyond your wildest dreams develop.

It will cost your company less money to hire a Sales Support Admin versus turning sales into miserable, sub-standard CRM administrators.

Mentor Tip for Fellow Sales Pros –
"You are A Sales Professional, Not An Admin."
~ Kimberlee Slavik, Author of Memoirs of An Angry Sales Pro – Sales Leadership MUST change!

I speak to readers of *Visnostic Sales and Marketing* every day and most of them know I am working on this book. As you can imagine, everybody has stories to share and this week, a salesperson forwarded an email to me that was so bad, it was humorous. When a sales leader sends out an email like the one I saw today, the message that it actually sends to the sales team is that the leader is under pressure and he isn't handling it well at all.

I won't go into all the details but this leader was driving people to fill out more and more in their CRM software. The jest of the requirement is that every salesperson must create a call plan for the week and upload it into the CRM tool. The target is 32 meetings per week. The time it takes to fill the call planner forms out and upload them, eliminates an entire day of selling.

But here is the dumbest part of this process; If a salesperson has a meeting and notices a potential new customer across the street, he or she better not go see them as a cold call because the system is setup to penalize any meetings that take place without a sales plan uploaded. Remember the chapter on "Compensation Drives Behavior?" Well technology mandates around reporting are creating the same exact type of havoc in the field.

This email about call planning not only disrupted salespeople from selling, guess what it created? Remember the chapter about "noise?" The last thing leadership should ever do is create noise in salespeople's head that distract from selling. What do you think this sales team did as soon as they saw the email? They got on the phone with each other and debated the content and the sanity of the leadership team.

Already these salespeople are calling recruiters to leave this administrative nightmare. Salespeople became salespeople to SELL. Sales leadership that has no clue how to be of value tends to over mange, micromanage, and over analyze to the extent that salespeople can't sell.

Look. I've BEEN this type of sales leader and I've made these same mistakes! And frankly, I get why leaders start acting this way. We aren't allowed enough time to sell with our teams! A sales leader is inundated with way too many internal leadership meetings. Because these meetings quickly fill up our calendars, there is no time left to spend in the field with the sales team. When this happens, those reports become a lifeline because that is the only source of information to answer any questions that arise during our meetings. And scheduling meetings with our team disrupts THEIR sales time!

STOP THIS MADNESS. Sales leaders often do things like this because we are also trying to survive the mandates put on US! But this behavior drives away the sales force.

And even if people stay, leadership will destroy the confidence of the sales team with this type of behavior. The best thing a leader can do when sales are down is to (how many times have I said this already?) **GET THEIR BUTTS IN FRONT OF THE CLIENTS ALONG WITH THE SALESPEOPLE!**

And while we are on the topic of technology, remember the story I told in Chapter One about the company that was **rumored** to have installed surveillance software on every company issued laptop? A salesperson that reported to me actually went off the deep end over his paranoia of being spied on. This is just another example of companies leveraging technology to make sales a more difficult job versus leveraging technology to make things easier on all concerned.

Lead by example. If you expect your team to have 32 meetings per week, fill out call planning reports, and upload and track it all in CRM, you better be prepared to prove it's even possible because if not, your team is laughing at you behind your back. And even if your ego can handle that, you have lost their respect and it will be almost impossible to inspire them.

Let us Sell. Go hire an administrator if that is what you really need. But turning salespeople into admins is about the dumbest thing any company could do to the sales organization. (Yes, I AM repeating myself….on purpose!)

CHAPTER 12 – Marketing & Sales Speak Two Different Languages – Vendor Speak versus Client Speak

NOTE - This is my favorite chapter because it is one of the most prevalent problems and yet it is the easiest to solve!

PROBLEM IDENTIFIED -

If you don't believe that friction exists between sales and marketing, you are either out of touch, in denial, or in the minority.

This is often a silent conflict and it is a revenue killer. Do your salespeople complain that they can't keep up with all the incredible leads they get from marketing or do they complain they don't get enough leads? When sales are down, which group gets blamed? Most of the time it is sales alone that gets beat up. Do you have an achievement club for sales? If so, how many marketing people also get recognized? If not, you may need to re-read Chapter Three. When sales increase, both groups believe they are the reason sales are up. Are they both being recognized? If not, resentment starts brewing. And if sales are down, are they both to blame? If both departments aren't involved in the problem identification discussion, how can they work together to fix poor sales?

PROPOSED SOLUTION -

Stop treating sales and marketing as two different organizations. They are the wheels and the tires of your company. They work best when balanced and when working in sync with each other.

When was the last time you invested in a team building exercise for these two groups?

I've worked for companies where sales and marketing were in alignment and I have worked for companies where there was a silent feud occurring that very few people were aware. When sales and marketing are out of sync and lack respect for each other, rarely will sales be healthy.

When I am conducting a Visnostic Translation workshop, I highly recommend that each company sends at least one representative from both sales and marketing. Whenever you have meetings involving decisions, it's imperative that both sales and marketing are included. During my workshops, it's been interesting to watch the relationships evolve. It's also interesting to hear the comments. Marketing usually says "This is the best marketing workshop I've ever attended." And Sales usually says "This is the best sales workshop I've ever attended." Then they both look at each other and stare. How can a workshop be perceived as both a sales and a marketing workshop? I believe that it's because they both contribute and they both see how their worlds will be impacted positively. Why more companies don't do this is a mystery to me but typically it's because those nasty politics get in the way OR a leader has made snide comments that impacts the way those teams view each other.

Come on Guys! We have to present this quarters sales numbers to the CEO!
SALES
MARKETING

We're deciding who takes the blame this time!

Collaboration and unity start at the very top. All levels of leadership must realize how powerful their comments are taken by those around them.

It's a huge burden to be a leader. Culture starts at the top and if leaders even HINT at anything negative about any of the organizations, the rest of the company responds with a negative reaction. There will be a distancing that naturally occurs. The old saying our parents taught us as children applies here in a very substantial way. If you don't adhere to this rule, leaders can cause irreparable damage:

If you don't have something nice to say about a department or employee, don't say anything at all.

PROBLEM IDENTIFIED –
Marketing thinks they create "tools" for salespeople. Yet they rarely ask sales what they really need. So these tools typically miss the mark.

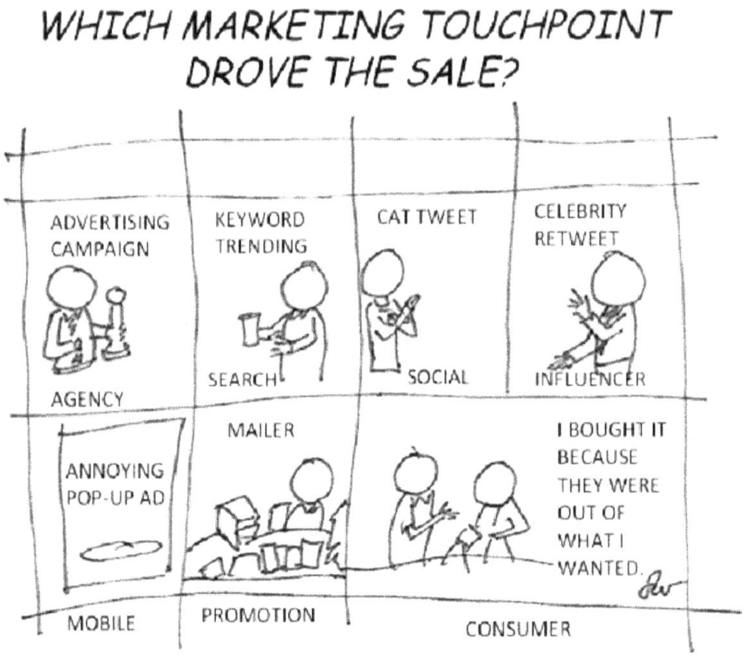

PROPOSED SOLUTION –
The right team building exercises can flush this out and improve communication. One thing that will surprise marketing is that sales does NOT consider your marketing toys, brochures, presentations, or website to be sales tools.

Sales should be treated as the customers of Marketing. And just as Sales needs to go talk to their clients to truly understand their needs, Marketing needs to talk to Sales to understand THEIR needs! Go talk to them and find out their challenges. You will be shocked at what they REALLY need and what little value your tools currently provide.

Does your company have a VP of Sales AND a VP of Marketing? Do they report to the same person? If you don't already have a Senior VP of Sales AND Marketing, please consider getting this very important job description written and hire someone both proficient in sales AND marketing! It's the best way to get these teams working together and LIKING it!

PROBLEM IDENTIFIED –
Sales and Marketing are often speaking two different languages.

Imagine for a moment that you go to school to learn Spanish and you become pretty fluent in the language. Then, before the big exam, your school sends you to France so you could practice speaking the language. However, practicing SPANISH in a FRENCH speaking country makes no sense, does it? This wouldn't exactly prep you for that big Spanish Test, would it?

Marketing Majors go to school to learn about buying behaviors. They learn about social media, promotional processes, retail, merchandising, fonts, colors and paper stock and study case studies of companies that failed and succeeded. This is a great education for HOW to deliver a message. This is the Spanish Language in the metaphor above.

Meanwhile, salespeople are out there with Clients (in France) and are presenting the company message in Spanish and are struggling on a daily basis trying to understand why they aren't making a connection with their clients. The problem is that sales is out there speaking VENDOR SPEAK (Spanish) and expecting their clients to TRANSLATE VENDOR SPEAK into CLIENT SPEAK (French)!

To add to this problem, not all vendors speak Spanish! Which means

Sales must determine what language they need to speak with each client! And very few clients have the energy, desire, or the experience to translate the VENDOR SPEAK into their own language. This is how your competitors beat you! THEY do a better job during the translation process!

The old adage, "Trash In Trash Out" is applicable with the marketing messaging. You can have the best-looking brochures on the planet but if its full of jargon, buzz words, and features and functions, you can throw it in the trash because it's often a foreign language to clients.

Sales needs content that actually TRANSLATES these features and functions into client RESULTS. If you don't know how to do this, please read Visnostic™ Sales and Marketing. It will change the way you view your content.

That's a great question. To be honest, I have no clue what I'm trying to sell here.

PROPOSED SOLUTION -

Stop talking like a Vendor. Stop expecting your clients to translate your marketing message into a language they understand! Vendors must start doing the translation from Vendor Speak to Client Speak!

One of the major differences between the top 20% of salespeople and the bottom 80%, is that the top salespeople INTUITIVELY know they have to do the translation for the clients!

Now what if Sales and Marketing started working TOGETHER to translate all the Spanish (VENDOR-SPEAK) into French, German, Italian, and all other languages too? To do this, sales will first need to figure out what language each client speaks!

Because communication breakdowns cause the most friction, relationships will improve dramatically once sales and marketing get on the same page and not only speak the same language, they AGREE on the language!

Visnostics™ has cracked this code!!! Visnostics (VISualization DiagNOSTICS) is the universal translator to help sales determine what language the client speaks and then provides the translation of their company's features and functions into a language that resonates and makes sense to the client!!!

Consider investing in a joint workshop between Sales and Marketing to TRANSLATE your marketing message (Vendor Speak) into Client Speak!

Please see the Workshops section of this book for more information.

CHAPTER 13 –
It's Really Hard to Be A Sales Leader. This Has To Change!

Mentor Tip for Fellow Sales Leaders –
MENTOR
Leaders don't create more followers. They create more leaders.

PROBLEM IDENTIFIED –
Most Sales Leadership Roles are destined for failure.

It is ironic that this chapter just happens to be #13. As I mentioned at the beginning of this book:

> **"My most secure jobs and my biggest paychecks have been when I was an Individual Contributor in sales. The least secure jobs and the smallest paychecks have been when I was a Sales Leader working the longest hours."**

Why in the world would anybody want to be a Sales Leader?

Sales Leadership MUST change!

During the past 12 chapters, I've shared leadership stories about politics, backstabbing, cussing, HR struggles, sexism, commissions and quota issues, firings, lawsuits, discrimination, and you will read in Chapter 14 about people that have actually DIED while doing my job!

You've heard that expression about poop rolling downhill? Well, as a Sales Leader, poop is coming at you from above, from below, and from all around you. No wonder why so many sales leaders are terrible leaders; they are a stressed-out mess!

Mid-level sales leadership is THE worst role ever! Most sales leaders don't even make it a full year these days. I reflect back and can see clearly now that several of my leadership positions were created specifically to be body shields for those above me. After all, when sales are down, someone has to take the blame. Who better than that first-line sales manager or VP of Sales?

As an individual contributor, when you perform, you should be safe in your role. But as a Sales Leader, you KNOW statistics prove that 80% of the sales force will fall short of their quotas Despite these proven numbers, you will still get blamed for the failure of others.

I made my first huge six figure commission working for David Wiener, the man that did all the artwork in my books. He taught me a LOT, which is why I still admire and respect him, and it is why we have continued to work together for years. David helped me be successful and then had to watch me make huge commissions, while his rewards were significantly smaller.

Instead of getting recognized proportionately for my accomplishments, he was beaten down daily because the other salespeople on my team were failing. He was one of the 7 sales leaders I mentioned that I had in just 5 years. David and Gary were the only two men out of those seven leaders that were actually GOOD leaders and both were abused and eventually fired – not for what THEY did, but because of what others did NOT DO! Both of these men were the only leaders that actually put their necks on the line to fight for their salespeople. The result is that they were loved and respected by their teams.

Keep in mind that David didn't hire any of those salespeople that were under performing. But he was blamed for their failures from his first day on the job. And if David had fired all of them and replaced them with a new, improved group of salespeople, do you think that would have saved his job? No, because the new people would have taken at least six months to ramp-up and get their feet underneath them. So either way, David was doomed due to the impatience, and frankly, the out-of-touch-with-reality Executive Leadership!

That is why sales leadership is so tough. Even a Great Sales Leader can teach and coach and help all day long but if the salespeople don't execute, guess who gets the brunt of the blame?

Why would anybody want a leadership role that was destined for failure? Who would want a job that would make less than the top individual contributors on the team?

ANSWER – Two very different types of Leaders:

1. People with HUGE Egos and
2. People that sincerely want to make a difference and care more about other peoples' successes than themselves.

So what do people with huge egos do when things start going bad? They start lashing out at their team. Thus, the cycle of abuse continues against salespeople. And what happens to the second type of sales leaders? They get abused by the executives and either leave for a better culture or they get fired.

And how are salespeople impacted by each leadership style? We either mourn the loss of the few good sales leaders we had, or we attempt to survive the abuse from the egotistical jerks that stay. All along, hoping that they too will get terminated before WE give up and leave. This quote is probably the most common post I see on social media:

People don't quit companies, they quite bad leadership.

PROPOSED SOLUTION –

How do we fix this? Well, I go back to the need for proper training and credentials in order to be a leader. Until a universal standard gets put into place, every company should take time to determine their specific expectations for every leader they hire. These expectations should be in writing, just like a job offer or a compensation plan, detailing what is acceptable behaviors and what behaviors will result in termination.

There needs to be a stronger effort at an Executive Level to avoid hiring politicians and self-centered leaders with egos. Do a better job vetting the candidates and eliminate those that will, without hesitation, throw their people under the bus to avoid taking accountability for their own failures and weaknesses.

Inspirational Quote -
It matters what leaders do or don't do

"The culture of any organization is shaped by the worst behavior the leader is willing to tolerate."

~Gruenter and Whitaker

But first, the hiring executives must admit if they have a bad attitude towards their own sales organization in general. As long as executives making the hiring decisions view salespeople and sales leaders as disposable and temporary, they will continue to make poor and sloppy hiring decisions.

I recommend that executives make a conscientious decision to NOT hire leadership roles that are intended to be body shields or token roles destined for termination. Companies should invest and commit to their hiring decisions. For example, many states today are "right to work" states, which means anybody can be terminated for any reason at any time. There needs to be a commitment from a company to allow a realistic amount of time for sales success to occur at all levels.

Most Executive Roles involve contracts that are similar to pre-nuptial agreements. These contracts guarantee executives a buyout clause in case things go awry. If they really mean what they say about having a sales friendly culture, signing an agreement with a sales leader guaranteeing him or her a realistic timeline to turn around or build a strong sales organization would be an outstanding first step.

When a company shows commitment and conviction to sales leadership hires, the culture SCREAMS that is has a sales friendly culture and does not view sales as a necessary evil.

By putting some skin in the game, a company will be much more careful to hire the right person.

And this contract should also spell out **consequences** for things such as ethics violations and other topics covered in this book.

By demonstrating a commitment to this level of leadership while clearly defining acceptable and unacceptable behaviors, these ground rules and rewards will setup a strong foundation for a long and successful professional relationship.

PROBLEM IDENTIFIED –
Sales Leadership is Not Empowered!

Sorry. I'm not laughing at your jokes. I'm laughing because you think I have enough authority to make a decision around here.

Duh! Empower them! This would be the obvious solution. Right? Easier said than done. Let me give some examples of things that have happened to me in various leadership roles:

1. I inherited a remote team located in different states. During my first week on the job, I attempted to schedule our first team meeting at corporate so we could meet each other and establish relationships and I could share my expectations and hear their concerns. This was rejected because the company didn't want to spend the money.

2. I put together a presentation and training for a day with a new sales team. When the CEO caught wind of it, he needed to see my deck and have me do a dry run before I was allowed to speak with my own people. He then sat in on the meeting and audited it. Why did you hire me if you didn't trust me from the

first day? By the way, this guy said he had a sales friendly culture; he did NOT.

3. I couldn't get travel approved to go visit a client. I had to go through a grueling approval process with lots of forms to fill out. This approval process took almost two weeks.

4. A CEO constantly called me and demanded I fire people that were about to make commissions. Over 40% of my time was spent with our recruiter attempting to keep my staff at full capacity. I couldn't keep up with the terminations and when I attempted to defend my team, it fell on deaf ears. It was obvious that the culture was a dictatorship; I was just a pawn with zero power to make my own decisions.

5. I worked for three owners and anytime I wanted to make any decisions, I had to go in front of all three of them and plead my case, which prevented any agility in the culture.

6. I ran a huge P&L (Profit and Loss) organization yet I couldn't get anybody to actually give me a budget! Instead, I had to build a case for every acquisition I wanted to make and present them to multiple people. I never knew how much I had to spend. So I had no clue if I was over or under budget until it was too late. Yet I was accountable for profits.

7. I had fundamental issues with a company that made my salespeople travel to various conferences and shows to work booths versus having marketing do this. Nobody cared about my experience or my reasoning why this made no sense. Even I had to do it. We did so many and traveled so much that our time for follow-up was almost non-existent. I never saw a deal close by having sales do this. Plus, this company had a huge turnover and having sales paraded at these shows just

amplified the attrition problem and hurt the company image. Nobody cared what I thought. Again, why did they hire me?

8. I was accountable for both sales and profit margins, yet my company hired someone in my territory and didn't tell me or have me engaged in the hiring process. So I was held accountable yet was not empowered to make decisions that impacted my compensation.

9. A company did three major reorganizations in just six months that disrupted sales efforts and morale. While I was in attendance of every planning meeting, it was obvious the decisions were made and nobody really cared if our leadership team agreed or disagreed with the details around the reorgs.

10. I've witnessed peer leadership come to the table with concerns, only to be terminated for expressing opinions. That didn't exactly inspire the rest of us to speak up. Instead, we all left.

11. I worked for a company that was very outspoken about being Christian based. However, part of this particular Christian culture also included the belief that women had roles and the input from women was not treated with respect. The number one revenue generator was a woman and she was constantly treated as an enemy and a threat. Instead, they should have promoted her to a partner level and empowered her as an owner. The original founders don't have confidence in women and it was blatantly obvious to everybody but them.

12. Regardless of which types of roles I've had, sales leadership was treated as a puppet versus a valued part of the team and organization.

I could keep going but I've probably already lost a few readers with the twelve examples I gave. Here is what is important - every example I just gave proved the assessment that each of these companies viewed sales as a necessary evil versus a valued part of the organization.

Ironically, most of these companies are out of business today, are struggling, or are experiencing stagnant growth and high turnover.

What is it going to take to open the eyes up to executive leadership that these behaviors, while many times are in place to control costs and expenses, are actually costing the company much more in the long run?

PROPOSED SOLUTION -
Empower Sales and trust their leadership. Set standards. Hire to those standards. Let them execute!

And be sure and read this book multiple times until it finally makes sense.

While it is going to take some time to establish standards and the proper collegiate curriculum and degree and certification programs, each company can start establishing their own set of criteria, leadership training, team building, and sales tools.

Don't put these things off because every single day is costing the company, the executives, the sales leaders, marketing, and salespeople money.

And if you haven't figured this out yet, leverage your salespeople to ensure you set the best criteria possible. They will be your best advisors!

Inspirational Quote –

There will be doubters.

There will be mistakes.

But with hard work,

There will be no limits.

CHAPTER 14 – Conclusion. Culture Starts at The Very Top - Sales is why everybody else has a job and C-Levels Need to Shout It From The Mountaintops!

This book was completed and the draft was distributed to a diverse group of people for feedback when I received a call from a former employee with some disturbing news. I had to add this story to the book.

He explained that gossip was spreading throughout his company about a co-worker of his that we both admire and respect. This Lady is beloved by those that report up to her and to her clients as well. She was extremely loyal and devoted to her company throughout her

11+ year career. Everybody could tell she loved her job and her company and that is a huge reason this company now generates almost one billion dollars annually today!

Recently, the owner of the company hired someone very similar to the Alec Baldwin character I mentioned at the very beginning of this book. This man declared war on her and she was quoted recently saying that the owner will either figure out the toxic nature of this new hire or he will be her demise. If the gossip is accurate, he won the war and she is now gone.

Bad leadership WILL destroy good leadership because good leadership is often viewed as weak and inferior. And bad leaders are notorious for believing that unethical behavior is admirable because it takes strong people to pull it off and get away with it. It's all about winning at all cost. (Like the kid that taught my son how to cheat. Yes, please tell me you figured out that story was another personal one.) So why would any intelligent company bring these types of people into a good culture?

This is what was explained to me regarding the reasons why most companies eventually migrate to an abusive leadership style: Companies go through phases and it is important that executives have the right types of personalities needed to push their companies to that next level of growth.

I actually believe there are legitimate points in this explanation. However, my observation is that changing to a more aggressive leadership style DOES work....but it only works **SHORT TERM**.

It's during this period of initial success that that dreaded **ENC Syndrom**e kicks in and executives become blind to (or they chose to ignore) the damage being done during this transition. Sadly, by the time they realize the destruction caused by the new leadership, it will be too late and the company brand, quality of employees, and loss of loyalty from clients will catch up with them. Unfortunately, by the time they figure all this out, it will be too late. Just think of all the companies you know that were on fire and are now gone or acquired.

If anybody is looking for a superstar with incredible ethics, let me know because this Lady will not be on the market very long! Their mistake will be another company's gold mine.

Remember the story I told about getting laid off Christmas Eve EVE (that's not a type-o) after blowing away our sales numbers? I mentioned that I often felt like I worked for Satan. I'm sure you all thought I was joking. In fact, I sincerely believe that if he ever got his hands on this book, he would know immediately which stories were about him and I can actually envision him laughing and enjoying reliving the stories I have shared. This man behaved as though he was at war with his employees. He viewed his tactics as brilliant and considered the way he mistreated his employees as smart business. He will be extremely proud to be part of this book! And he will convince himself that I'm just too stupid to appreciate the genius behind his behavior.

That's the thing about bad leadership; bad leaders typically have enormous egos and are therefore blind to the errors of their ways. They are oblivious to the destruction they cause because they see everything they do as their personal victories. And they are completely clueless how much it actually costs them and their company when they abuse employees. But what this man did to me was nothing compared to what happened to two (that I know of!) other people that worked for him.

After I left, I was no longer able to protect my team and one of the men that I hired was found dead in his hotel room.

It took several months for them to reorg again and resurrect my old role. They hired a man to replace me. He was only in my former position for a few months before he was also found dead in his hotel room.

The details around their deaths are not important here. The point is that both men were employed by, traveling for, and died while working at this company. And they were both YOUNG! The culture of this company literally kills people. What type of advice can I possibly give to address this?

I want the PUBLIC to think we are a super chill and positive company. But I want YOU to think of us as the company that will destroy you and your family if you screw up.

The only response I can think of is quite lame; "Don't work for companies like this!" This sounds so logical but it's not as easy as it sounds. I know that both men that died knew this company was not right but they didn't quit. In fact, I knew it was a terrible company but they had to reorganize and lay me off for me to leave! Why do we stick with jobs that we know are bad for us? The answer for me personally is that I know every time a salesperson or leader leaves a company, it is assumed the sales professional failed. Very few people ever consider that **the company might have actually failed the employee!**

This is so cliché but culture starts at the very top. And if the people at the top of the food chain think sales is a necessary evil and the company punching bag, there is nothing anybody can do to change this culture. If you are a leader and you sincerely want to change your attitude towards sales, let's discuss ways you change your behaviors:

First of all, accept that it's going to be difficult for any employee to completely trust a company enough to be brutally honest about what they think and what they observe. They want to continue to get that payroll check each pay period. Therefore, if you REALLY want to know what is broken, bring in a fractional leader to evaluate the situation.

When you hire fractional leadership, pay them upfront. That may sound insane (cost-of-money would justify dragging out payment to vendors) but it's actually much better business than it may first appear; I watched one of the big accounting firms bring in fractional leadership and their OWN goal was to replace as many permanent employees with their consultants. There is an excellent book called, *Dangerous Companies* that exposes the tactics of the big firms. They are not very different from permanent employees; they also want those checks to come every pay period BUT they also want to grow their business by increasing headcount and dragging out their projects. Beware of temporary employee business models like these.

Instead, hire a fractional leader for a month. Pay him or her upfront. Put that expiration date in a contract so it's very clear that this is a limited engagement. Spell out exactly what you expect for that fee you are paying and then let them get to work. As long as they know they only have a specified amount of time to deliver specific results, you will take away any hidden agendas and defuse the desire to drag out the process in order to bill you more. You must include in the contract that if they don't get the job done in the agreed upon timeline, they must continue to work for free until they provide an acceptable deliverable. What is it going to hurt to at least try this?

While this external hire is uncovering what is broken, you can focus on your permanent, internal team. When was the last time you tried to catch sales doing something right? I wish every sales leader at every level would make this a goal every single day. The life of a salesperson is brutal. It is hard to get rejected almost every single day of your career. We need encouragement, understanding, compassion, loyalty, and RESPECT.

I worked for a company that had THE highest turnover I have ever seen in any sales organization. The leader seemed so genuine during the interview process because he took complete accountability for the failure of the previous sales regime. THAT is extremely rare! But once I was on board, it didn't take me long to observe the CEO slamming the previous salespeople to other employees. It's a well-known human trait that if someone talks poorly about another person, the chances are extremely high they will do the same thing to you.

So when I started feeling excluded by other leaders in the organization, I sensed it had begun. People from other departments I eventually started telling me what was being said. One of the absolute worst things a leader can do is talk bad about an employee and that employee hears what is said by anybody other than the leader that said it. Trust will be obliterated and that trust cannot be restored. And this damage is not just with the person that is being slandered; few people realize that the people HEARING senior level executives talking bad about other employees or past employees are also affected negatively. The smart ones know that it's just a matter of time before they become the topic of slander as well.

Mentor Tip for Fellow Sales Leaders –
CHOOSE YOUR WORDS CAREFULLY
If you don't have something nice to say about your department or employee, don't say anything at all!

CEOs that have not been salespeople will often have little understanding or respect for sales. These types of leaders tend to put way too much emphasis on marketing and are often oblivious to how little the sales organization benefits from what marketing is doing.

Once again, who does an employee turn to for advice when this happens? HR? Where does HR go for advice and guidance? Are we supposed to believe that HR won't go to the CEO with the concerns? I worked for one company that the HR department was the daughter of the owner. Nobody felt comfortable talking to her about ANY issues. The result is that employees will continue to leave instead of giving input that could potentially help fix what is broken. If they can't see that having the owner's daughter in charge of HR is discouraging open and honest feedback, maybe they aren't as smart as they think they are.

When you see a sales resume full of successful quota attainment but a high turnover rate, before you throw that resume in the trash, consider the stories I've shared with you in this book. You may be throwing away a resume of one of the most ethical and professional candidates you've ever considered. With the right culture and a professional attitude towards sales, this person may spend the rest of his or her career exceeding revenue objectives and being grateful for finally finding decent leadership. I admit that I have a soft spot for these types of candidates because they tend to be extremely grateful, are extremely loyal, and have incredible work ethics.

This is the final mentor tip for Sales Pros and it is the most important one:

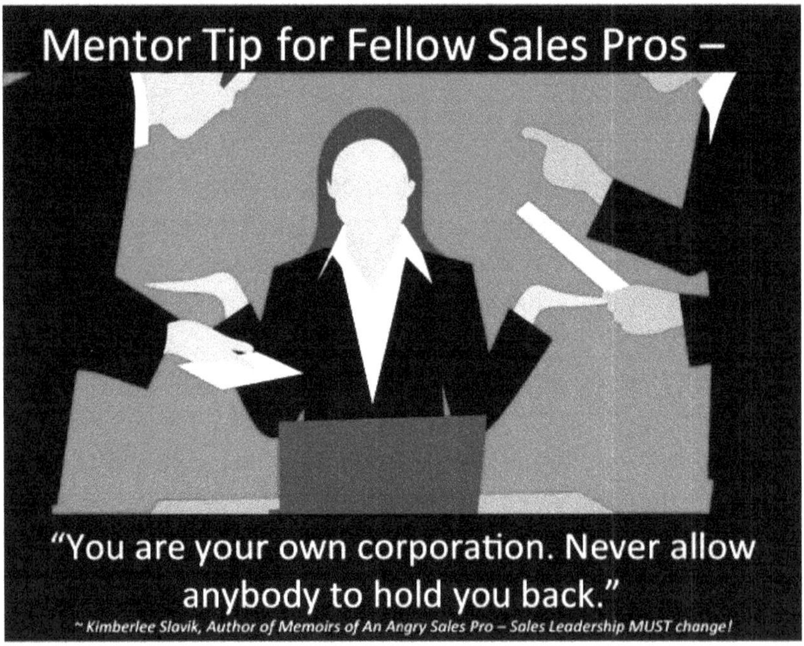

Mentor Tip for Fellow Sales Pros –
"You are your own corporation. Never allow anybody to hold you back."
~ Kimberlee Slavik, Author of Memoirs of An Angry Sales Pro – Sales Leadership MUST change!

Sales is tough and you deserve to be respected for what you endure each day. Be sure you represent our profession with dignity and class. What you do and how you do it, is a reflection on YOU and only YOU.

Are you getting up and working an honest day? Do you deserve to be respected by your leadership? Are you doing something that helps you grow every day? Do you support other salespeople? Do you have a mentor? Do you mentor someone? You truly are your own corporation. People can take away your job but only you can give away your integrity or reputation. Protect it. When you are gone, it is the only thing of value you leave behind that matters. And it's fragile. You can work your entire career and have a pristine track record. However, one detour down the wrong path could result in that mistake becoming your legacy. Guard your reputation carefully.

And this is the final mentor tip for Sales Leaders:

Mentor Tip for Fellow Sales Leaders –
BE A GOOD ROLE MODEL
"It is not what we do that makes us great. It is how we impact those around us that makes what we DO great!"
~Kimberlee Slavik

As a Sales Leader, what do you want your brand to be? Have you looked at your LinkedIn profile lately? How many of your former salespeople have written recommendations on your leadership abilities? If you don't have very many, you may want to do some self-reflecting. I have found that salespeople that admire and respect their leaders will write recommendations without even being asked because they want to work for them again someday.

Do you really think you impress anybody when you mistreat your people? How many topics in this book struck a nerve? Have you started planning how you are going to change your behaviors towards those that need your leadership the most?

What have you done to improve your own skills? Companies no longer reimburse leaders for continuing their education but that shouldn't stop you from making efforts to become a better leader. When was the last time you invested in your own education? How many associations are you active that can help you become a better leader for your team? Are you sure your standards are high enough as you hire your staff? Is your attrition high or low? What are you doing to retain your current team? A GOOD Sales Leader is hard to find. Make it a goal to be someone's "Unicorn."

And finally, to the Executives reading this, are you using your sales leadership as a body shield? Are you throwing them under the bus with investors when you fall short of your projected earnings? Why not just take accountability and put a plan in place to fix things instead of constantly rebuilding your sales organization? If they are falling short, what can YOU do to better to support them and help them be more successful? Have you brought in third parties to give their unbiased assessment of your current sales processes and team?

When was the last time you sponsored team building exercises? Do you have members of sales on your advisory board? If so, do you have both weak and strong salespeople represented? Often, the weak ones have valuable insight that could turn that bottom 80% of your salespeople into top performers. What have you done to help drive the need for credentials for sales professionals? Do you have a healthy culture that supports sales and marketing working together or have you unintentionally pitted them against each other? Are there silent battles taking place that you are unaware? What about the "silent chaos" I described? Are your employees currently struggling with any noise? Have you leveraged fractional sales leadership to help you uncover those hidden obstacles that internal people don't want you to know? When was the last time you went on calls with the salespeople in your organization? Have you become overly dependent upon reports to tell you the story about your business? And are you sure you have the right people in leadership roles? Are you sure you don't have those dreaded politicians blocking you from knowing what you need to know? I'd love to help you figure all this out.

I've spent my entire career looking for a company that respects me. I've dreamt of a company that appreciates and is in complete alignment with my ethics, morals, and integrity. I've searched for an offering that actually worked. In fact, I'd rather sell the most expensive software, service, or product as long as it was the BEST innovation around. I've looked for a strong sales culture and leadership that I admire and can continue to learn and grow professionally. This book is a compilation of the results of those efforts and it's been a pretty interesting journey. I've definitely grown just as much from the bad experiences in my career, as I have the good ones. But I often wonder how many years the bad experiences have shaved off of my life.

I hope this book sheds some light on the things that MUST change in order for sales to become a more attractive career path for future generations. I don't think Millennials or Generation Z will tolerate the treatment that I've described in this book.

I look forward to hearing from readers about what topics they would like to see added in the next edition.

Good people are out there. Resumes don't always tell the whole story. If we are going to make sales an honorable career path, Sales Leadership AT ALL LEVELS MUST change!

And that change must start with YOU!

Inspirational Quote –

"Almost every successful person begins with two beliefs:

The future can be better than the present,

and

I have the power to make it so."

~ David Brooks and Kimberlee Slavik

APPENDIX –

Podcasts and Other URLs:
Visnostic Podcasts, Education, and Speaking:

July 19, 2019 – Donald C. Kelly, The Sales Evangelist
The Fundamentals of Visnostic Selling
https://www.stitcher.com/podcast/donald-kelly/the-sales-evangelist-sales-trainingspeakingbusiness-marketingdonald/e/62674347

June 18, 2019 – Brian Burns, The Brutal Truth About Sales Basic Visnostics – Statements NOT Questions
https://www.stitcher.com/podcast/brian-burns/the-brutal-truth-about-sales-selling/e/61931321?autoplay=true

April 22, 2019 – Dr. Pelè, Big Ticket Clients
Basic Visnostics
https://www.youtube.com/watch?v=FbW-sSu4BOo&t=304s

Current CEO DynaExec Introduction to Visnostics
https://player.vimeo.com/video/353714183

Memoirs Content Reference:

DiSC Training
http://www.metamorphosiscct.com

Glengarry Glen Ross Clip
https://www.youtube.com/watch?v=Q4PE2hSqVnk.

Top 25 Business Books
https://www.businessinsider.com/best-selling-business-books-bill-gates-warren-buffett-2018-1

What bad behavior like sexual harassment costs
https://www.marketwatch.com/story/as-harvey-weinstein-takes-a-leave-of-absence-heres-how-much-sexual-harassment-costs-companies-and-victims-2017-10-07

Buy Books:

Memoirs of an Angry Sales Pro – Sales Leadership MUST Change!
https://www.amazon.com/Memoirs-Angry-Sales-Pro-Leadership/dp/1733194630/ref=sr_1_1?keywords=memoirs+of+an+angry+sales+pro&qid=1568169902&s=gateway&sr=8-1

Visnostic Sales and Marketing
https://www.amazon.com/dp/1733194622

Visnostics Special Edition for Real Estate
https://www.amazon.com/Visnostics-Neuroscientific-Approach-Communicating-Marketing/dp/1733194614/ref=sr_1_2?keywords=visnostic+selling&qid=1566930437&s=gateway&sr=8-2

Visnostics Special Edition for Auto Sales
https://www.amazon.com/Visnostics-VISualization-DiagNOSTIC-Neuroscientific-Communicating/dp/1733194649/ref=sr_1_3?keywords=visnostic+selling&qid=1566930437&s=gateway&sr=8-3

Kimberlee Slavik:

Connect and message on LinkedIn
https://www.linkedin.com/in/kimslavik

Author Page
https://www.amazon.com/Kimberlee-Slavik/e/B07NCK2353?ref=sr_ntt_srch_lnk_1&qid=1566929596&sr=8-1

Company and book sites:
www.dynaexec.com
www.visnostics.com
www.visnosticselling.com

David A. Wiener:

Connect and message on LinkedIn
https://www.linkedin.com/in/david-a-wiener-573b1a1/

David's artwork
http://artbydavidwiener.blogspot.com

WORKSHOPS

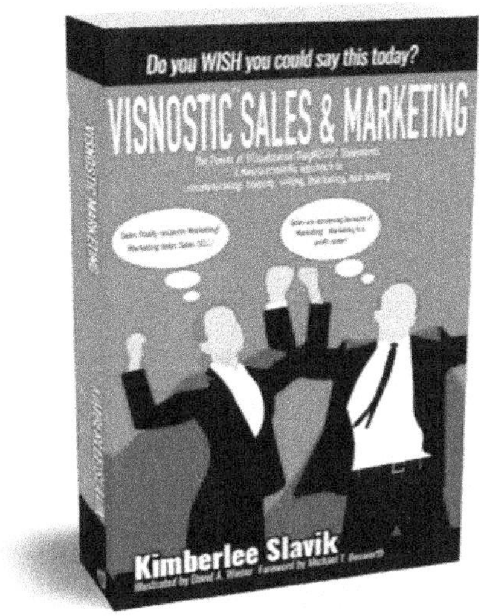

In addition to Fractional Leadership that can be contracted for a day, week, month, quarter, or an entire year, there are three workshops that help DynaExec clients execute three major principles taught in the best-selling book, *Visnostic Selling* (replaced with *Visnostic Sales & Marketing*).

First, vendor-centric marketing messaging must be translated and converted into client-centric Visnostic Statements. This is accomplished by working with sales and marketing during a ***Translation Workshop***. This is the fundamental workshop needed to create stronger messaging. This workshop eliminates the need for clients to translate features and functions and other jargon into "why they care." This is accomplished by doing the work for them. This workshop converts current messaging into dialogue that will improve your clients' comprehension and retention of your messaging.

In addition, you will strengthen your rapport with your clients because they will FEEL positive emotions while engaging with your sales organization. Your sales organization will be able to quickly identify the clients' non-strength areas in which your company can convert to strengths.

Once the translation is completed and 10-20 strong "Visnostic Statements" are created per segmentation, the next step is the ***Solution Mapping Workshop***. This second workshop is conducted with a more technical team while reviewing the Visnostic Statements created during the Translation Workshop.

Often, these second sets of eyes will identify and create additional Visnostic Statements to the ones Sales and Marketing identified during the Translation Workshop. In addition, this second group tend to enhance the newly created statements with powerful results they have observed during their post sales efforts. These final Visnostic Statements are then mapped to various Statement of Work descriptions that will describe HOW any "non-strengths" uncovered during the client discussion can become strengths. These Statement of Work descriptions are created during the Solution Mapping Workshop.

The final stage of the Visnostic transformation is to take the Visnostic Statements and the Statement of Works and complete a tool that will be given to the entire sales organization. Imagine a sales team that is in front of the client with a tablet, documenting the client responses. And residing on the tablet is a tool that will automatically produce an "Insight Report" that will give your clients a recipe for success INSTANTLY!

This will eliminate the need for technical resources to be engaged early in the sales cycle. The client will see exactly how your company will turn their non-strengths into strengths!

The third workshop is ***Visnostic Selling***, which is conducted with the entire sales organization to ensure they are each experts with the tool and they are well prepared to properly engage with the client.

Your sales organization will be CONFIDENT and COMPETENT in front of potential clients from their first WEEK in their sales role!

Here are the three workshops in greater detail -

★ *Client-Centric Translation For Sales & Marketing*

Objective –
Conversion is a form of translation. Converting features and functions into VISualization DiagNOSTIC (aka Visnostic) Statements is the act of translating vendor-centric wording (vendor-speak) into client-centric statements (client-speak) that clients can relate. DynaExec will assess current marketing tools & combine details from multiple sources to create Visnostic Statements & compatible visuals & graphics that enhance retention.

Attendees –
Sales and Marketing (Up to twelve participants)

Pre-requisites, Planning, and Preparation for Workshop –

- **Read *Visnostic Selling* Book** – (Preface, Chapters 1-3) Retail Price - $24.95 Workshop Discounted Rate - $19.95
- **Meeting #1** – Assessment - Conference Call to hear Presentation & Record for transcription (obtain script)
- **Meeting #2** – Assessment Results Revealed. Kick-off conference call after book is read but prior to workshop to set expectations

- **Meeting #3** – Onsite 8-hour Translation Workshop
  - ✓ CHAPTER ONE – Believing is Doing and Introduction (30 minutes)
  - ✓ Exercise #1 – "XXXX" exercise.
  - ✓ Slide presentation using graphics vs words
  - ✓ 3 graphics versus letters exercise – 3 seconds per slide Generation Z get timer added to PPT
  - ✓ CHAPTER TWO – Segmentation and why it is important. (30 minutes)
  - ✓ CHAPTER THREE – Solution Dissection. (1 hour)
  - ✓ CHAPTER FOUR – Translation (1 hour)
  - ✓ CHAPTER FIVE – Creating & Rating Visnostic Statements with Post It Notes by Segmentation. The importance of RTH. Use highlighters to identify, Reword if necessary. Prioritize. (1 hour working lunch)
  - ✓ CHAPTER SIX – Vertical and Target Market Strategies with Visnostic Statements (1 hour)
  - ✓ CHAPTER SEVEN – Class Presentations. Time will be determined based upon number of companies in each session and flexibility of class.
  - ✓ CHAPTER EIGHT – Conclusion and discussion of two additional workshops to create the tool. Demo of tool.
- **Ongoing Meetings (up to 30 days)** – Ensure success and document results are included in the workshop price.

Supplies Needed for In-Person Workshop –

- Conference Room with projection and white board
- Phone for call-in participants
- Internet
- Post-it Notes supplied by DynaExec
- Highlighters supplied by DynaExec

★ *Mapping Segmentation Solution Workshop for Post Sales Roles*

Objective –
After the feedback from the client is collected, a deliverable must be created that maps all "NON-STRENGTHS" identified with Visnostic Statements. It is important to not simply map products or services names to the areas in which can be strengthened. This workshop will summarize HOW your company will help clients improve their current situations. The result will be a client deliverable called an Insight Report.

Attendees –
Technical Team such as Software Engineers, Implementers, Support, Compliance, etc. (Up to twelve participants)

★ *Visnostic Sales and Marketing Workshop*

Objective –
After the first two workshops, a sales tool will be completed that converted features/functions and other technical jargon into statements the client can reflect and visualize. Sales will learn how to deliver this approach in lieu of a traditional sales presentation. Sales will learn how to use the new tool designed to create the Client Insight Report. Sales people need to be entertained to learn. This workshop will have games and prizes as a shorter version of both previous workshops is conducted to ensure the sales organization understands basic Visnostics and the science behind why it works so well.

Attendees –
Sales and Sales Leadership (Up to twelve participants)

In less than 30 days and three workshops, with Visnostic Selling, your sales, marketing, and leadership will be transformed into Client Business Strategists. Furthermore, your clients will no longer avoid your teams' sales efforts because they will be viewed as a valuable extension of your client's own teams.

★*Additional Information*

Workshops can be conducted in public forums or in private sessions.

The benefit of group forums is that during your presentation to the group, you will be educating other companies on the benefits, results, and differentiators of your company, which could result in new clients.

TIP – Companies that send representatives from both marketing and sales will benefit the most from the Translation Workshop, which is the most popular and fundamental way to strengthen the effectiveness of the messaging.

★*Assessment of Current Messaging – Pricing Options*

ASSESSMENT - $1,500
This includes approximately 10 hours of consulting work prior to the in-person workshop. Cost of the Assessment will be applied to any future consulting services and workshops.

1. Read at the minimum, Preface and Chapters 1-3. (2 hours)
2. Record your best presentation (30 min max) on Zoom with slides.
3. Transcribe the presentation. (3 – 5 hours)

4. Bring four different highlighter pens (blue, yellow, pink, and green are preferred).
5. Be prepared to discuss your top five differentiators over your competition. (1 hour of research)
6. Download app – Poll Everywhere

POST WORKSHOP - $500/month retainer for consulting services.

Visnostic Sale and Marketing Readers and Pod Cast audience may contact podcast@DynaExec.com for ***a free assessment ($1,500 value).****

When was the last time you purchased a $25 book and received $1,500 of consulting for FREE?

***Special Pricing is for a Limited Time Only**

BIOGRAPHIES

Author Bio and Resumé

Kimberlee Slavik –https://www.linkedin.com/in/kimslavik

Kimberlee is an award-winning business strategist in the Information Technology (IT) industry, known for helping clients increase sales and profits by leveraging software, services, hardware, storage, business continuity, & cloud computing.

Currently CEO of DynaExec.

Results:

- ✓ Best Selling Author and inventor of Visnostics
- ✓ Sold or participated in selling over $1.9 billion worth of complex enterprise software, products, & services during a 30-year career
- ✓ Exceeded quota for 26 years of a 30-year career averaging almost 200% of plan
- ✓ Award Winning Global Sales Leader
- ✓ Over 85 unsolicited recommendations on LinkedIn from clients, peers, direct reports, indirect reports, and management validating accomplishments
- ✓ Dozens of 5-star book reviews describing reader successes
- ✓ Exceeded $900 million-dollar revenue objectives while leading a 70+ person storage team with P&L accountability for HP
- ✓ Recipient of numerous sales awards by focusing on post-sales support and customer references
- ✓ Set sales records that have not been broken in over 20 years

Specialties:

- ✓ Surpassing sales objectives
- ✓ Expert at selling intangible offerings
- ✓ Excellent post-sales client relationships
- ✓ Member of multiple advisory boards
- ✓ Training and education development and execution
- ✓ Transforming salespeople into top performers
- ✓ Exceptional business acumen & P&L (Profit and Loss)
- ✓ 15 years of people leadership
- ✓ Excellent communication & presentation skills
- ✓ Key Note Speaker
- ✓ Collaborative team player leading multiple teams towards a common goal
- ✓ Project management & organizational skills
- ✓ Organizational design & coaching high-performance teams
- ✓ Enterprise channel strategy development & execution
- ✓ C-level executives & senior execs sales closures
- ✓ Indirect enterprise channel sales & marketing
- ✓ Expertise in technology – including SaaS (Software as a Service), cloud, storage, virtualization, & business continuity

Education:

- ✓ Summa Cum Laude from LeTourneau University, with a Bachelor of Science degree in Business Administration.
- ✓ Certified by Southern Methodist University in "Leading the High-Performance Sales Organization."
- ✓ Currently pursuing an MBA degree in International Business at Heriot-Watt Business School in Edinburgh, Scotland.

Foreword Bio and Resumé

Artist Bio and Resumé

David A. Wiener – https://www.linkedin.com/in/david-a-wiener-573b1a1/

David is an action-oriented generalist with diverse sales and marketing experience in high technology environments. After engineering design and system installation of cryogenic systems, he entered the selling world of investment brokerage of large apartment buildings.

Then, after a decade of real estate investment, he moved to the high-tech industry. He has a strong focus on business start-up, market expansion, and turnaround situations. He demonstrated success in sales and sales management of system and application software as well as hardware. He has been successful at small and large companies and divisions of large companies starting new ventures. He has held positions up to and including VP Sales. He has held a TS clearance and has expertise with systems integrators and government programs.

After his career in high tech, David moved on to small farm communities in Florida, Texas and then upstate New York where he built a studio and produces his art of fine ink drawings, oil paintings, and ceramics. He also spends his time working for his town as chair of the planning board. He also is a member of the County planning board and a board member of the town fire department.

Education: Newark College of Engineering - BSME, MSIE, MSCIS (abt)

For more information about David's artwork or to commission his talent, please visit http://artbydavidwiener.blogspot.com

YOU

www.ingramcontent.com/pod-product-compliance
Lightning Source LLC
Chambersburg PA
CBHW070248200326
41518CB00010B/1739
* 9 7 8 1 7 3 3 1 9 4 6 3 1 *